P9-EDT-293

Gail Culbertson
Rauh

Sexuality, the Bible, and Science

Sexuality, the Bible, and Science

by Stephen Sapp

FORTRESS PRESS   Philadelphia

Library of Congress Catalog Card Number 76-62617

ISBN 0-8006-0503-9

6192L76   Printed in U.S.A.   1-503

To
JAMES H. PHILLIPS

friend, mentor, colleague, and the person most instrumental in arousing and encouraging my interest in the academic study of sexuality—

in gratitude for the contribution he has made to me and to so many others in our understanding of sexuality, and especially of Christian marriage.

Contents

Preface

Religion has long been a major influence upon human self-understanding; science has rapidly become an equally—if not more—important factor in contemporary determinations of who we are. This
book arose from a concern that these two approaches seem to have less
and less to say to one another in the realm of sexuality, an aspect of
human existence that has become most crucial to many people today
in the definition of their humanity. If one assumes (as I do) that religion and science are both concerned with reality and seek Truth—
albeit in quite different ways—it follows that they should not have
mutually exclusive or antagonistic understandings of what it means for
men and women to be sexual creatures. This book presents an approach which brings together the views of both religion and science
into a contemporary Christian interpretation of sexuality.

I have limited my consideration of religion to the Judeo-Christian
tradition, and a word is in order about my use of the Bible. I have
tried, as a Christian ethicist, to be responsible to the Bible (as the
source for Christian theology and ethics) without pretending to be a
biblical scholar and becoming overly preoccupied with technical questions of exegesis. That is, I have used the results of biblical research
to inform my theological-ethical constructions. What I have attempted,
therefore, is theological reflection, not exegesis, and I have taken certain
biblical passages as paradigmatic or illustrative of my theological
points. I have tried to avoid the extremes of forsaking the Bible completely and doing theology in a vacuum, and of getting so involved in
the exegetical task that I am unable to do theology. In short, I have
attempted to take seriously, and to be responsible to, the Bible as the
informing and guiding source for my theological-ethical reflection.

Furthermore, I have selected those passages in the Old and New
Testaments which seem most relevant to an understanding of sexuality
as such, not necessarily to the development of practical guidelines for

behavior. This is an essay in Christian ethics, not morals; my concern throughout is primarily to reach a Christian understanding of sexuality which is viable today, not to describe the ways in which that understanding might be applied to specific problems or situations. Chapters 1–4 represent my attempt to distill from a vast amount of biblical research those elements which are most helpful in this task.

The biological sciences are now providing the most important scientific contributions for our understanding of sexuality; much of this research has implications for sexuality that will make oral contraceptives and abortion "on demand" seem minor issues by comparison. Chapter 5 reports some of the biological findings which are most directly relevant to the task at hand. For reasons that will become apparent, however, it is impossible to limit to biology the scientific contribution to the question; Chapter 6, therefore, presents the significant aspects of a reexamination of the "nature-nurture" debate from the perspectives of psychology and cross-cultural anthropology.

With the presentation in the first six chapters of the results of my research in the biblical and scientific fields, I have chosen the dialectical view of reality set forth by William Temple as the most useful framework within which to bring the two views together in the final chapter. Temple's thought in many areas is rich with meaning for us today; and his "dialectical realism" is especially appropriate in the realm of sexuality as an antidote to the extremes to which both science and theology have been—and are—prone. There may be other ways to overcome the apparent gap between science and religion on this issue, but I do not know of one that offers more promise or that is more in keeping with the Judeo-Christian understanding of man.

Acknowledgements are such a routine part of every preface that they sound almost automatic and therefore perhaps trite; this situation, however, makes each writer's expressions of gratitude no less sincere. There are many people to whom I offer my deepest gratitude, but the following merit special mention: Harmon L. Smith; Robert T. Osborn; James H. Phillips; and my students in "Christian Marriage and Family" and "Religion and Human Sexuality" at Duke University, for their guidance, suggestions, stimulation, and encouragement; Julie Hillebrand, for her cheerful assistance and efficiency in the final preparation of the manuscript; and the person who has shared most deeply every aspect of this endeavor—my wife Mary. It is very difficult for me to distinguish between those ideas that are mine and those that are hers; perhaps, finally, that is a distinction which cannot be made in a marital partnership as close as ours. Her encouragement has rejuvenated my flagging motivation more than once, and her love has sustained me constantly.

Stephen Sapp

Note: I am sympathetic to those of both sexes who are troubled by the generic use of the pronouns *he, his,* and *him,* as well as of such nouns as *man* and *mankind* to indicate the entire human race, and I am sensitive to the issues involved. I have made an effort to avoid such usage wherever possible, but there are many places where clarity of expression and economy of language simply outweighs whatever benefit would be derived from the avoidance of this admittedly unsatisfactory trait of the English language. I hope that the *content* of what I have to say about the role and status of women in these pages will not be overlooked because of the linguistic *form* in which some of it must be expressed. Anyone interested in this issue would profit from a reading of *Language and Woman's Place,* by Robin Lakoff (New York: Harper & Row, 1975), especially pp. 43–50.

1

Old Testament Foundation: The Genesis Creation Accounts

The goal of this book is to reach an understanding of human sexuality that takes into account recent contributions of the biological and social sciences and at the same time incorporates those insights into human nature which are found in the Judeo-Christian tradition, specifically in the Old and New Testaments.

Before we examine the Old Testament statements about human sexuality, however, several comments are in order. In the first place, with respect to the passages to be examined, of necessity I have been highly selective. The Old Testament contains many references to sex and sexual behavior, and it is clearly impossible even to mention all of them here. I have chosen only those passages that seem most important and most worthy of detailed examination for their contribution to a *definition* of human sexuality.

Furthermore, specific laws concerning sexual behavior, of which there are many in the Old Testament, are considered generally insofar as they illustrate this larger view. We cannot be concerned with exegetical details but rather shall try to review the contributions of biblical scholarship in an effort to grasp the broad sweep of Old Testament teachings about what it means to be a sexual being.

The Separation of Sexuality and Divinity in Yahwism

One aspect of Israelite religion merits particular attention because of its underlying importance for an understanding of the Old Testament attitude toward sexuality: The firm conviction of God as "Other"—as Creator clearly distinct from his creation—is strongly evident in the religion of ancient Israel, despite its obvious anthropomorphisms. That is, if God created the world by mere verbal command (or, for that matter, by fashioning some material with his hands), as claimed by the Genesis creation stories, then he is radically different in

1

nature from it. This understanding of God is especially important
because it represents one of the most significant differences between
the world view of the Hebrews' ancient neighbors and that of Israel.
Given the religious environment in which Yahwism arose, this departure from the prevailing pattern of thought had a profound impact
on Israel's attitude toward human sexuality.

The Canaanite Baal cults were fertility religions which celebrated
creation as the result of the union of male and female deities. This
view of creation as procreation is not surprising, given the crucial place
of fertility (and by implication, sex), in an agrarian society, nor is it
unusual that the archetype for the "human" sexual relationship was
seen to be a sexual relationship in the divine realm. Thus the logical
assumption arose that human sexuality was also divine, to be used in
the worship of the gods as imitative of their own mysterious creativity.
Despite the strong influence of these cults, as far as the Hebrew God
was concerned, "any thought of sexuality in him, or of his acting in
creation by means of sex, was completely alien to Israel."[1] There was
no sexuality associated with God, no female consort or goddess at his
side, and therefore no creation by divine begetting of offspring.

Thus, in early Hebrew religion the concept of divine fatherhood
was separated from that of human, physical fatherhood. Although
man was created in the image of God, he was not born of a sexual
union. To become a son of God was not the result simply of a physical relationship but rather that of a spiritual one. Admittedly, there
are numerous examples in the Old Testament of the constant failure
of the Hebrews to abandon the prevailing belief in a sexual god and
his goddess,[2] but these lapses do not negate the fact that Yahweh is
consistently portrayed as needing neither consort nor progeny to perform divine acts.

Of course, one cannot go to such an extreme as to deny totally any
concern about fertility in Yahwism. To ancient man the gods were
the source of life and fertility, and if Yahwism had not been a fertility

1. Gerhard von Rad, *Old Testament Theology*, I, D. M. G. Stalker, trans. (New
York: Harper & Row, 1962), 146; hereafter cited as *OTT*, I.
2. The Canaanite fertility goddess Asherah is mentioned over forty times as a
temptation to the Israelites (as, e.g., in 1 Kings 15:13 and 2 Kings 21:3, 7),
and the prophets speak out frequently against Israel's tendency to forsake
Yahweh for the fertility cults (cf., e.g., Jer. 44:15–23).

religion, it would have been useless to the people. What distinguished the Israelite religion from other contemporary religions, however, was the separation of sexuality from divine creation—i.e., the demythologizing of fertility discussed in the preceding paragraph. By his Will alone, God had created *in the natural order* the processes by which fertility was assured, and agricultural success therefore could not be coerced or stimulated by imitating the supposed divine fertility (which itself, of course, was denied) through ritual sexual activities.[3]

In short, although there are undeniable similarities of language and form between the Genesis creation accounts and the myths of the fertility cults of the time, a very different view of the relationship between God and man is presented by each. The biblical stories were not intended to be recited in a magical fertility ritual: Rather than indicating how God can be forced to fulfill human needs and desires (as he is through magic), the Hebrew accounts of creation show the total dependence and responsibility of humans before the God who created them.

The implications of this view for one's understanding of human sexuality are profound, one of the most important of which is the placing of sexuality totally within the realm of creatures. For the Hebrews, the archetypal sexual partnership was no longer divine but human, the prototypal couple no longer a god and his consort but two created beings. This represents, as Joseph Blenkinsopp says, "a positive demythologizing and desacralizing of sexuality," and the "function of human sexuality in the society is no longer derived from mythical archetypes but from reflection on experience."[4] The distinction between the sexes is a *creation* by God since there is no such distinction on the divine level; the polarity of the sexes belongs to the created order and not to God. Hence, this distinction becomes one of the major qualitative differences between man and God.

Furthermore, sexuality is removed from the realm of those demonic and impersonal forces which man can attempt to placate through proper ritual activities but against which he is ultimately powerless.

3. Walter Harrelson, *From Fertility Cult to Worship*, Anchor Books (Garden City: Doubleday & Company, Inc., 1969), pp. 10, 54.
4. *Sexuality and the Christian Tradition*, (Dayton, Ohio: Pflaum Press, 1969), p. 25.

Sexuality becomes an element in human life over which man does have control (however difficult it may be), and thus a major step is taken toward a genuinely personal existence, especially vis-à-vis sexual relationships. This "radical departure . . . from the general trend of thinking" in antiquity is illustrated in the Old Testament, according to Blenkinsopp, by the adultery of David and perhaps preeminently by Joseph's rejection of the advances of Potiphar's wife. Although the stories have different endings, both clearly indicate that man is responsible for how he uses his sexuality: To borrow from a different context, the "demon" of eros may be "couching at the door . . . but you must master it" (Gen. 4:7).[5]

This radical exclusion of sexuality from divinity (or vice versa) may appear to imply a negative value judgment of sex by the Old Testament. In fact, there is near unanimity among scholars that exactly the opposite is the case, even to the extent that several recent commentators suggest that the only hope of rescuing the Christian attitude toward sex is a complete return to the ancient Hebrews' healthy, positive understanding. It is central to our task, therefore, to examine the reasons why Yahwism considered human sexuality as essentially good despite its sharp separation of sex and divinity.

This quest logically takes us to the beginning, and we shall now look closely at the Old Testament's presentation of creation. Since one's understanding of sexuality is inextricable from one's understanding of man—an observation as true for the ancient Hebrews as for us— any attempt to uncover the roots of the Old Testament's view of sex must take into account the broader question of the nature of man. Nowhere in the Old Testament is this interrelationship more clearly depicted than in the creation accounts of Genesis. Hence, it is to an examination of some of the central concepts of Genesis 1–3 that we shall devote a major portion of this investigation of the Old Testament view of human sexuality. As we do so, it will become apparent how Israel's unique view of her God and the nonsexual quality of God's role in creation influenced her accounts of the origin of man and of his nature as a sexual being.

5. *Ibid.*, p. 28. For an interesting treatment of the theme of *responsibility* as a major component of creation (i.e., Wisdom) theology, see Walter Brueggemann, *In Man We Trust: The Neglected Side of Biblical Faith* (Richmond: John Knox Press, 1972).

Man as a Psychophysical Unity

Our comprehension of the creation accounts of Genesis will be enhanced if, before examining them directly, we consider briefly one aspect of the Hebrew view of man, namely, the concept of psychophysical unity. This idea almost certainly would have been held by the authors of these accounts, and it would have played an important part in their understanding and presentation of man's creation. In discerning what they were trying to express in the Genesis narratives, we shall be aided by a prior knowledge of the anthropology that had developed by the time they wrote. And what is of special importance to us is that, far from considering man in terms of the body/mind dualism of Greek philosophy, the Hebrews conceived of man as a psychophysical unity.

It is difficult for those who have been educated in a tradition that considers the "soul" to be the "real person," and the body to be merely a necessary and troublesome encumbrance, to comprehend this concept; but familiarity with the Old Testament notion of man as a psychophysical unity is necessary not only in order to understand the Genesis creation accounts but also to interpret some of the New Testament statements about sex. The concept will also play a role in our later effort to reach a viable contemporary understanding of sexuality.

Although the Old Testament speaks of man's "flesh," "spirit," and "soul," it does not depict these as separate substances that only coincidentally or unfortunately cohere but as interdependent elements that are necessary for human existence. The *nephesh*, or "soul," rather than being a distinct immortal entity, is actually the "life principle," the individual's vitality, or that which is alive. Thus the mental and physical activities of the individual are merely different manifestations of the same underlying "living being." Clearly, then, the "body" in the Old Testament is not seen as a prison from which the soul struggles to escape: A person simply perishes if the body and soul (or spirit) are separated.

This belief is well illustrated by passages such as Job 34:14-15 and Psalm 104:29-30, and it is further supported by the lack of a doctrine of personal immortality in the Old Testament: The "soul" is not preexistent and does not survive the body. So inextricably are they united that when the body dies there is nothing left as a separate entity to pass on to another existence. The Hebrew notion of psychophysical unity means therefore that instead of *having* a body, a human being *is* body: The individual is a vital body, the manifestation in flesh of vitality. The soul does not have a body but rather is a body that is alive. To use H. Wheeler Robinson's felicitous terms, a human being to the Hebrews was both an "animated body" and an "incarnate soul." In short, the person does not exist apart from the body, which is the outward manifestation of the total reality that includes it.

From a contemporary Western perspective, this is a rather materialistic view, which is not surprising given the nature of Old Testament religion; but it is not, I think, simply materialistic. Rather it serves to balance the emphasis in Western thought upon the intellectual or "spiritual" as the only truly valuable dimension of human existence (a view which, incidentally, calls into question the worth of sexuality). The sum of the matter, then, is that even if the "soul" (whatever it may be) were the ultimately valuable element, it cannot function in this life without the body, which is the essential means of self-expression.

The P Account

The first three chapters of Genesis, as is well known, actually contain two accounts of the creation of man: The first, 1:1–2:4a, from the Priestly source (P), and the second, 2:4b–3:24, from the Yahwist source (J).[6] It is generally accepted that P received its final form after the Exile (ca. 500 B.C.), although it contains a great deal of much older material, and that J was written some four to five centuries earlier (ca. 950 B.C.), making it the oldest narrative source in the Old Testament. This difference in date of composition, along with the different purposes of the authors, helps to account for certain discrepancies and emphases in each of the stories which will be important in our interpretation of them. This is not the place, however, to enter into a description of the characteristics of the two accounts.[7]

6. The question of the "mythological" character of these stories, although an important and interesting one, is beyond the range of our interests. As we examine these accounts of the origin of man and the sexes, the profound definition of myth offered by the noted evolutionist Theodosius Dobzhansky suggests the proper perspective for our inquiry; he observes that myths portray "things which never happened but always are." See *Mankind Evolving*, (New York: Bantam Books, 1962), p. 228. For the sake of convenience, the two stories will be considered in the order in which they appear in the Bible.
7. Concise, helpful summaries of the major differences between the J and P sources may be found in the following: Gerhard von Rad, *Genesis: A Com-*

The Image of God in Man

One of the most striking statements in the creation story which appears first in Genesis (the P account) is that "God created man in his own image" (1:27). Since the Hebrews did not attribute sexuality to their God, it is especially important for us to ask what the priestly author meant by man's creation "in God's image, after his likeness." Given Yahwism's prohibition of "graven images" (Exod. 20:4), P's use of the expression "in God's image" is surprising since the phrase could be interpreted in a literal sense. The use of the two words here, though, probably indicates that the author was aware of this problem and wanted to make certain that such a literal misinterpretation would not occur. So, instead of using *image* alone, P added another word to show that a very special kind of image was meant, i. e., a *likeness* or *reflection*. The somewhat vaguer connotation of the second word protects against an overly concrete, material interpretation of the first.

The priestly author did not mean to imply, therefore, that it is in God's *physical* image that man was created, and God's image certainly means more than that man looks like God or members of the heavenly court. The word *image* more likely implies likeness to God in that man possesses the capacity to think, to communicate (with his fellows and with God), to act self-consciously, perhaps preeminently to *respond* to God's will for him. Claus Westermann pointedly asserts that we cannot in any way "objectify" the image of God in our description of it: The phrase "really means that God has made man to communicate with him, so that man might speak to God and he might hear God's word."[8] Image therefore means that man reflects God's nature, that he possesses qualities similar to God's. This special endowment, the exceptional method of man's creation (the pattern of divine command is broken for a divine resolution), and the dominion granted to man over the rest of creation all contribute to an emphasis by P on man's uniqueness and special relationship to God.

---

mentary, John H. Marks, trans. (Philadelphia: Westminster Press, 1961), pp. 23–27; hereafter cited as *Genesis*; and E. A. Speiser, *Genesis*, Vol. I of the Anchor Bible, William F. Albright and David N. Freedman, eds. (Garden City: Doubleday & Company, Inc., 1964), xxiv–xxix. Each of these works also discusses characteristics of the sources throughout the commentaries on specific passages, as does von Rad in *OTT*, I, especially 136–151, and Harrelson, *From Fertility Cult to Worship, passim*.

8. *The Genesis Accounts of Creation*, Facet Books (Philadelphia: Fortress Press, 1964), p. 21; hereafter cited as *Genesis Accounts*.

As was just mentioned, the priestly author was careful not to allow his use of the phrase *image of God* to be interpreted too literally, in violation of his religion's prohibition of "graven images." Unfortunately, in traditional Christian interpretations, this concern has been carried to an extreme, and the phrase has been totally spiritualized and intellectualized. The result, of course, is that human physical existence, and sexuality in particular, have been excluded from likeness to God and thus disparaged. It is to this situation, especially relevant to our task, that the Hebrew concept of psychophysical unity can contribute a needed corrective.

This notion of the organic unity of the human being precludes the view that P intended any spiritualization of his idea of human creation "in God's image." That is, since pure spiritual being (as well as its qualities or attributes) did not exist for the Hebrews apart from some form of material manifestation, the image of God must apply also to man's physical body. Von Rad clearly rejects those interpretations which result from an anthropology alien to the Old Testament and view God's image in man as purely spiritual: "The marvel of man's bodily appearance is not at all to be excepted from the realm of God's image."[9] This of course is not to exclude man's spiritual nature, which we have just seen was surely the major component of the image of God for P. Rather it is merely to insist that man's physical being, as an *inseparable* part of the total entity called man, does share in the likeness.[10]

The words *image* and *likeness*, then, refer to man in his totality, encompassing both his material/bodily and his spiritual/mental components.[11] In short, the whole person is created in God's image and therefore comes under the divine judgment of "very good." Nor is there any hint in the P account that "image" refers to an original righteousness or innocence that humans possessed at creation but lost

9. *Genesis*, p. 56.

10. Lest there be misunderstanding on this point, a distinction drawn by von Rad is crucial. It is true that the Old Testament can be quite anthropomorphic in its depiction of Yahweh. But, according to von Rad, we tend to interpret this in exactly the opposite direction from what the Old Testament meant because "it cannot be said that Israel regarded God anthropomorphically, but the reverse, that she considered man as theomorphic." See *OTT*, I, 145. That is, we must start *from* God and not from man when we consider "God's image" in man.

11. This view gains strong support from Gen. 5:3, where the identical words, though in reverse order, are applied to Seth's resemblance to his father Adam, which clearly refers to bodily form as well as spiritual nature; cf. 5:1.

by later disobedience.[12] If we interpret the word *image* in the meaning which it had for a fifth-century Israelite priest, we recognize that human bodily form—and hence man's nature as a sexual being—was in part what was meant.

In summary, the image of God in man, in addition to a concrete reference to man's bodily form, seems to have been P's attempt to express whatever it is that makes man different from the rest of creation, that makes him "human." Man, unique among all the animals, has the option of responding to God's will for him positively or negatively, i.e., of obeying or disobeying. Thus, we can affirm that man's creation in God's image confers upon him uniqueness and dignity by virtue of his special relationship with the Creator and the authority given him over the rest of creation; but this authority simultaneously demands a certain responsibility in man's use of it, a notion which is vividly portrayed in the J account. Before we examine J's presentation of the creation, however, several other features of the P version merit attention.

The Necessary Relationship of Male and Female

The Hebrew word for "man", *adam*, used in both creation accounts is neither the proper name Adam nor a collective which emphasizes men as a group; it is rather a generic term, in the sense of *mankind* as distinct from the animals.[13] *Adam* most definitely does not refer to man as a male biological creature, distinct from woman; to make this distinction, the word *ish* is used, as in Genesis 2:23. When the priestly writer says, "So God created man in his own image," there is no question that woman is included, as the conclusion of the same verse (1:27, "male and female he created them") makes clear (cf. Gen. 5:1-2).[14]

12. Von Rad agrees, citing the same passage about Adam's begetting Seth "in his own likeness after his image" referred to in the previous note. God thus authorized man to pass on his "image," which is man's supreme dignity, in continuing procreation of the generations. So it cannot be said that the image of God is lost, especially since it is appealed to in Noah's time (Gen. 9:6b). See *OTT*, I, 147.

13. N. W. Porteous, "Man, Nature of, in the OT," *The Interpreter's Dictionary of the Bible*, K–Q (New York: Abingdon Press, 1962), 243; hereafter cited as *IDB*.

14. This same wording precludes the possibility that P had in mind any sort of androgynous creature as often found in other creation myths, perhaps most eloquently in Plato's *Symposium*. For the author of the P account, the first human was not a male/female who was later separated, perhaps as the result of some type of sin.

It is also significant that, in contrast to the J account, man and woman are created simultaneously in P with no hint of temporal, much less ontological, superiority. Further, the blessing of fruitfulness and dominion is delivered to both male and female together, which appears to be P's short-hand way of expressing the same basic notion as J's famous description of woman as a "helper fit for" man.

This suggests a major conclusion to be drawn from the P creation story: The "image of God" refers neither to Adam alone nor to Eve alone, but only to the two of them together, to the "them." About P's presentation of the creation of male and female in 1:27–28, Johannes Pedersen says,

> Singular and plural are used indifferently about the same being. Man is a whole consisting of two parts, the man and the woman. Nothing is said of the relation between them, except that they are indispensable to each other, and not till they are united do they together form a whole human being . . . the man and the woman together make man.[15]

Whatever idea P had of the nature of man, it seems clear that for him this idea necessarily included male and female, not male alone. P seems to be saying, therefore, though in less picturesque and more abstract terms, exactly what J had said before him: God's creation of mankind was not complete until *both* man and woman had been created and the two brought together in what is by definition a sexual relationship.

It is therefore clear from a reading of the very first chapter of Genesis that the Old Testament faces the question of sexuality directly, as a basic fact of creation to be accepted, not hidden. By presenting man's creation as male and female, P assured that sexuality must be seen as an intended part of human creation in the image of God. God did not make a "mistake" in creating sexuality, nor did it arise as a punishment for man's sin. Rather, P says, God intended it from the first and consciously willed it as an essential aspect of human existence.[16]

---

15. *Israel: Its Life and Culture*, 1–2 (London: Oxford University Press, 1926), 61–62.

16. Although it has been effectively obscured by the traditional misinterpretations, the J account clearly corroborates P's unequivocal statement that God intends sex from the beginning, that he chooses deliberately to make man a sexual being: Both male *and* female (and therefore sexuality!) are intentionally created by God before any hint of sin, of whatever kind, enters the picture.

What is crucial is that sexuality is presented as fundamental to what it means to be human and therefore must be taken very seriously. There is no creation of humanity in general and only later a differentiation between the sexes, but from the beginning P can speak of mankind only as male and female. Furthermore, when God has completed his creative work, he pronounces the judgment "very good" on *all* of it, including the sexuality of man. In short (as we will see more fully when we consider the Song of Songs in the next chapter), since Yahweh was a loving God, everything he created, including human sexuality, was good and to be used and enjoyed responsibly. This attitude of course precluded belief in metaphysical dualism (which views the world and the body as evil), a fact that will be important for our interpretation of the New Testament understanding of sexuality.

Sexuality as a Divine Command/Blessing

That P understood the relationship of man and woman as sexual is clear (apart from the mere fact of the existence of male and female) from God's first words to his new creatures. He commands male and female to exercise the sexuality he has created: "Be fruitful and multiply." Besides being a command, there is also an element of blessing in these words, which is to be repeated whenever the promise of great achievements is bestowed (cf., e.g., Gen. 9:1; 12:2; 17:2–6; 22:17). In keeping with the Hebrew separation of sexuality and divinity discussed above, it is interesting to note, as von Rad does, that this procreative ability is not seen as a manifestation of or emanation from man's creation in God's image. This, of course, is to be expected precisely because of the view of Yahweh as creating by his Word rather than by sex. What is significant and lends even greater honor to the place of sex is that man's ability to procreate is clearly separated from God's image and given a special blessing as a distinctly creaturely activity.[17]

There are two aspects of this understanding of God's blessing that are worthy of note. First, as indicated above, the blessing patently supports the contention that sexuality is part of God's good creation. Indeed, the words have somewhat the sound of a blessing that could be part of a wedding ceremony, and there is certainly no hint that the necessity and desirability of procreation arose as punishment for hu-

17. *Genesis*, pp. 58–59.

man sin. Instead, procreation is presented as a normal and intended part of the "good" creation. Second, the divine blessing precludes from the outset any notion of human sexual activity as dirty or evil because such activity becomes the very means commanded by the Creator himself to carry out his will for humanity. Indeed, this divine command/promise played a central role in the Old Testament attitude toward sexuality since it led the Hebrews to consider the propagation of their race as one of their main goals in life.[18]

The J Account

The author of the J account told his story in a very different way from the priestly author, though both were concerned to describe the creation of man in the sexual duality of male and female. From the restrained, precise formulas of P, it is quite a step to the detailed personal narrative of J, and one of the most striking things about the J account is the important role played by the woman. Indeed, it is possible to argue that the woman's role is more important than the man's in both chapters. This may seem to be a strong statement given the current opinion that J's presentation of the creation of woman (and Paul's use of it!) is the *locus classicus* for the birth of male superiority and the subjugation of women. Nevertheless, the claim for the woman's centrality in the story has much to recommend it, and a reexamination of some aspects of the J account will not only allow a possible reappraisal of this issue, but will shed considerable light on our general topic.

The Equality of Male and Female

As we have seen, P makes no distinction between male and female in terms of importance and thus indicates that God did indeed create them equal. J, because of the temporal priority assigned to the male's creation, has usually been interpreted as implying thereby an ontological superiority also.[19] But it is not unreasonable to suggest on the

18. The difference between the Hebrew view of the relationship of divinity and sex and that of the fertility cults needs to be reiterated here. For the Baalists, sex was divinely ordained as an imitation of the way in which the gods themselves created. For the Hebrews also, sex was divinely commanded, but it was seen as one's contribution to the possible redemption of one's race because, as God's chosen people, every Hebrew male carried the seed of Abraham, from which the Messiah would come.

19. This same argument, if applied to the P account, would of course mean that "every living creature that moves" (not to mention light, the seas, vegetation,

contrary that the whole story seems to build to an intended climax in the creation of the woman, whose elaborate creation is in marked contrast to the relatively perfunctory creation of the animals (and even of the man himself! Cf. 2:7, 19 with 2:21–23).

It is significant that the words translated by the RSV as "helper fit for him" (the infamous "helpmeet" of the KJV) actually have a rather different connotation in the original Hebrew: Their literal meaning is "alongside him" or "corresponding to him," with the notion of similarity as well as supplementation. Von Rad, stressing J's presentation of the kind fatherliness of Yahweh, even considers the creation of the woman as "the last and most mysterious of all the kindnesses" of Yahweh to the man: "She was to be like him, and at the same time not identical with him, but rather his counterpart." Von Rad approvingly quotes Delitzsch, who renders the notion "as the mirror of himself, in which he recognizes himself."[20] The New English Bible captures this same emphasis and provides perhaps the best translation of the concept in simple English: God provides "a partner for him." Genesis 2, then, presents woman as man's partner and therefore implicitly his equal. It is crucial to note that only in Genesis 3, *after* the sin of disobedience—when the state of existence God had intended for his creatures has been disrupted—is woman seen as subordinate.[21] Thus, whatever the traditional interpretation, it appears that J considered the original state of creation to have been somewhat different, though since disturbed by sin.

The Necessary Relationship of Male and Female

We have seen that for P the image of God clearly consists of and requires both male and female. A similar notion is present in J and is of considerable importance for an understanding of human sexuality.

---

etc.) is superior to man since they were created first; and in the J story itself, the human female would have to be seen as inferior to all the rest of the animals. Not surprisingly, however, those who are eager to apply this reasoning to the male-female relationship in J are much less willing to be consistent and apply it to P and to the female-animal relationship in J as well.

20. *OTT*, I, 149; *Genesis*, p. 80.

21. Cf. 3:16, which, taken in context, J surely means descriptively, not normatively. This verse, often cited as proof of the divinely ordained superiority of the male, is actually a condemnation of it (after all, it is itself in the context of a curse, not a statement of how things should be!). The dominance/subservience model is clearly a *result* of the Fall, with its disordered relationships, and thus not God's will but the very thwarting of it. Genesis 3:16 therefore can hardly be appealed to as God's ordination of female subjugation.

Here again J seems to provide details omitted by P's theological reticence, an amplification perhaps intended by the final editor in his arrangement of the three chapters. Throughout the P account, each act of creation is judged "good," with the total creation (including human sexuality) characterized as "very good." The only place in the whole presentation of creation where the judgment "not good" is pronounced is in 2:18b: "It is not good that the man should be alone."

We see here corroboration of P's contention that man by himself is less than human, that he needs another in order to reflect truly God's image and to fulfill God's purpose. And this other is *woman,* the only companion really "fit for him." Again, in different terms and with different emphases, "male and female he created them." J does not imply inferiority by having woman created last, but rather just the opposite: Until the woman is created, the man is incomplete and "alone," without suitable companionship. For J as well as for P, then, true humanity exists only in community, and the fundamental form of this community for both authors is the relationship between man and woman. Again, sexuality—human existence as male and female—is strongly affirmed as a central element in God's intention and plan for mankind.

The essential nature of this duality is shown by the fact that God creates the woman for the man even though the relationship itself becomes the vehicle for human disobedience. Even with this consequence, nevertheless it is not good for the man to be alone! God's providential concern for his creatures allows them to experience intimate relationship, even if such relationship is the arena for temptation, disobedience, and separation from him.[22] In fact, this view finds indirect support in the story of the original disobedience itself: Only after *both* had eaten did anything happen. There is no indication whatsoever that Eve was affected until Adam too had disobeyed (cf. 3:6–7: "And she also gave some to her husband. . . . *Then* the eyes of *both* were opened"; italics added). Here is a very practical illustration of the true unity of male and female before God: Not only did creation lack fulfillment before both sexes existed, even disobedience was incomplete until both disobeyed!

The reason given by J for the creation of woman—that the man should not be alone—is also important to our inquiry. Although the

22. Westermann, *Genesis Accounts,* pp. 29–30.

physical aspect of the sexual relationship cannot and should not be denied, it is interesting that, even with the Hebrew emphasis on procreation, J stressed man's *loneliness*, his need for a companion worthy of him, as the immediate reason for woman's creation. There seems to be more implied by this wording than the mere satiation of sensual desires. Indeed, that the woman was created solely to fill the man's sexual needs is unlikely because the animals were created as the first effort to satisfy the perceived lack. And there is simply no hint in the text that the animals were to serve any sort of sexual function, but rather one of companionship and aid, despite the claims of some commentators to the contrary.[23] The animals failed in this task, and only with the creation of woman did man recognize the companion "fit for him." J seems to be saying once again that only in relationship with someone who is his equal does man enter into a fully human existence. And this relationship, although physical satisfaction and perhaps even procreation are important aspects of it, contains considerably more than either of these.

The Purpose of the J Account

This emphasis on the necessary partnership of man and woman suggests that Genesis 2—3 may really be an account of the creation of the sexes rather than merely of mankind, with an additional explanation of the basis of the current relationship between the sexes. This interpretation is in keeping with the generally recognized etiological purpose of J, one of the main aims of which is the explanation of the

23. On pp. 33–35 of *The Creation of Woman: A Psychoanalytic Inquiry into the Myth of Eve* (New York: McGraw-Hill Book Company, 1960), e.g., Theodor Reik cites such a view set forth by Morris Jastrow in "Adam and Eve in Babylonian Literature," *The American Journal of Semitic Languages and Literatures*, XV (July, 1899). Jastrow claimed that the original idea of the Genesis account is that man forsook his animal companions only after finding a partner "worthier of him." His position is based on the affinities which Genesis 1—3 shows with Akkadian mythology, in which the hero Enkidu happily copulated with his animals until seduced by a harlot; after a week of mating with her, he returned to the animals, but they would have nothing to do with him. I find no trace of this idea in Genesis 2, however, and with good reason. To take the position that God originally intended the animals to be the man's sexual partners is simply to make the text bear more than it can, especially when we note that J wrote in the midst of Yahwism's struggle for survival with the pagan fertility cults, one element of which was the divinization of animals and their possible use in fertility rituals (cf. Exod. 32:1–10). J was too staunch an adherent of Yahwism to have intended any suggestion that Yahweh could ever have entertained the notion of animals as appropriate sexual partners for man.

origin of the two sexes and their unquenchable drive for union with each other.

It is interesting to note that there is no mention at all of children in this story, indicating that for J God's creation of sexuality was to serve purposes other than mere procreation, as was discussed in the preceding section. J apparently wanted to explain why a man and woman forsook blood ties (of incomparably greater importance in J's time than in ours) and entered into a relationship with each other based on a love that was stronger even than that of a child for its parents. He found his explanation in the fact that eros, the inextinguishable desire of the sexes for each other, was given to man *by God himself* in the creation of woman from man (cf. "therefore" in v. 24). According to von Rad, this fact "gives the relationship between man and woman the dignity of being the greatest miracle and mystery of Creation."[24] Furthermore, this eros is presented not as appropriate only in Paradise and certainly *not as a result of sin* (Ch. 2 comes *before* Ch. 3!), but as a permanent and intended aspect of human existence resulting from God's purposeful design. This view—that God willfully created the desire of the sexes for each other—sheds considerable light on a further aspect of the J account.

The Knowledge of Good and Evil

The concept of the "knowledge of good and evil," including the notions of nakedness and man's first disobedience, is important to us, because it bears upon the question of whether sex was really intended by God in the creation of humanity. In the P account, we have seen that God clearly wills man to be a sexual being from the beginning, and he gives as his first blessing and command that man should exercise his sexuality. Concerning J, however, and despite the evidence already presented that J held the same view as P, there is much less agreement among scholars. Some (including von Rad, e.g.) claim that Genesis 3:1–7 presupposes an ignorance about sex on the part of the humans that is overcome only after they eat of the tree of the knowledge of good and evil.

In general, there seem to be two schools of thought on the meaning of the "knowledge of good and evil." One holds that the Hebrews

24. Von Rad, *OTT*, I, 150.

used *good and evil* not in a narrow moral sense but to mean "everything," with such knowledge therefore signifying omniscience in the fullest sense of the word.[25] In the morally based Hebrew culture, then, *good and evil* would have been a natural phrase to designate the two extremes of existence between which everything falls, much as we in our intellectually based culture might say, "He knows from A to Z." The other position maintains that this view is untenable on the basis of biblical usage elsewhere and of comparative religion and mythology, and that the only interpretation validated by Genesis itself is that "knowledge of good and evil" means consciousness of sex. Thus, when Adam and Eve "were both naked, and were not ashamed," they were without knowledge of sex, and they recognized their nakedness and felt shame only after eating the fruit. Shame, then, is closely associated with sexual consciousness.[26]

We cannot consider the detailed arguments offered by the proponents of each side of this debate, but two points can be made in response to the second position presented above. It is clear from the temptation story that God (or members of the heavenly court) possessed the "knowledge of good and evil." This, in fact, was the serpent's argument for eating the forbidden fruit, in order to be "like God, knowing good and evil" (3:5). And it appears that such knowledge was the result, since in 3:22 (an admittedly difficult verse) God says, "Behold, the man has become like one of us, knowing good and evil." We need not reiterate here the earlier discussion of Yahwism's radical separation of sexuality and divinity. It is sufficient merely to reaffirm that one of the distinctions of Hebrew religion was, as Martin Buber put it, that its God was "supra-sexual,"[27] creating merely by divine will rather than by sexual coupling with a female deity. Thus it is very hard to see how the "knowledge of good and evil"—a specific possession of God in this story—could possibly have been sexual experience or consciousness.

Furthermore, those who equate "knowledge of good and evil" with

25. A fuller presentation of this view is found in George Wesley Buchanan, "The Old Testament Meaning of the Knowledge of Good and Evil," *Journal of Biblical Literature*, 75 (June, 1956), 114–20.

26. For a thorough study of this position, see Robert Gordis, "The Knowledge of Good and Evil in the Old Testament and the Qumran Scrolls," *Journal of Biblical Literature*, 76 (June, 1957), 123–38.

27. *Good and Evil* (New York: Charles Scribner's Sons, 1953), p. 71.

consciousness of sex contend that the lack of shame about being naked means that the first couple were not conscious of their sexuality. Such a position assumes that sexuality itself occasions shame by its very nature (once one is aware of it). But this suggests that sexuality was *not* part of God's intention for humans in creation, whereas we have seen that *both* creation stories consider sexuality to be a purposeful part of God's good creation, with no indication whatsoever that sexual experience was jealously withheld from Adam and Eve.

An interpretation of the story which is more consonant with Hebrew attitudes toward sex, especially as they are presented in Genesis 1 and 2, would hold that the sin of the first couple, far from being sexual in any sense, was one of *pride,* of overstepping the limits God had placed upon them as finite creatures (symbolized by the forbidding of the one tree) and attempting to become "like God" (or "gods"). The Bible throughout considers pride to be the root and essence of all human sinfulness, and there is every indication that this story is no exception. Here we have a graphic depiction of the first instance of man's *hubris,* of his attempt to set himself up as his own "center of value," and his refusal to accept his finiteness and limitations.

The consequences of this prideful attempt to usurp God's place are important to us: The man and woman disrupted their relationship to God (symbolized by their expulsion from the Garden) and thus to the rest of creation (cf. 3:15–19), with the result that their own relationship with each other was disordered. The woman became subservient and the man dominant, neither a healthy position to occupy, and neither God's original intention for the male-female relationship, as we have seen.

A further, and not surprising, result of these disrupted and disordered relationships was a sense of *shame* at the intimate exposure of their "nakedness" to God as well as to each other (3:7). But it is crucial for us to understand that the shame referred to here was not meant to be sexual at all (though our society seems incapable of not equating shame with sex and physical nakedness automatically). Instead, "nakedness" is a powerful symbol for having one's weaknesses exposed, a vivid sign of shame and dishonor, of helplessness and vulnerability before a more powerful and righteous authority. Shame, in essence, is a response to being unmasked, to being "made naked" in a figurative sense, to being, as we might say, "caught in the act." Thus the point which the biblical author wanted to convey by his use of the image of "nakedness" would be better understood today (and with far less damage to Christian views of sexuality) if Genesis 3:7a were translated, "Then the eyes of both were opened, and they knew they had been caught *with their pants down!*"[28] The imagery is the same, but the point is much clearer to us.

In short, that the man and the woman were naked and not ashamed before the Fall does not at all imply that they were unaware of their sexuality, or that it came into use only after their disobedience. The entire Hebrew attitude toward sex, as well as certain aspects of J's method and intent, offers strong presumptive evidence to the contrary, namely, that, before the disruption of man's disobedience, sex was a perfectly natural and accepted aspect of man's created nature. The traditional Christian interpretation, then, is a misinterpretation because it is untrue to what the text says in its Hebrew context within the Old Testament. The explanation for this misinterpretation may be found in the Genesis story itself: It is impossible for us to imagine sexuality without some sense of shame precisely because we live in the disordered state after the Fall![29]

It cannot be denied, of course, that P accepts sexuality as an intended part of creation much more easily than J, and this discrepancy may be attributable to their different times of composition. As we have seen, Yahwism waged a long struggle for survival with the various fertility cults of Baal, and J probably wrote during this conflict. Baalism promised its worshipers a share of the divine prerogative of creation through ritual coitus, whereby they became masters of the force of life; such mastery is basically what the serpent promised. J does not fail to take this opportunity to point out the result of such attempts to arrogate to oneself what should be God's: Far from the

---

28. I am indebted for this idea to Henricus Renckens, *Israel's Concept of the Beginning: The Theology of Genesis 1—3* (New York: Herder and Herder, 1964), as I am for several other points throughout this discussion.

29. One further objection to this interpretation—that there is no mention of sexual activity until after the first couple have been driven from the Garden (4:1)—is easily explained by J's purpose and narrative style: He first had to relate the creation of man and woman and their disobedience before it made any sense at all to talk about the rest of history, which required the begetting of offspring by Adam and Eve—he was merely telling a story in its chronological sequence. Thus, the fact that the narrative is silent about sexual activity before the Fall is no more proof that it did not occur than silence about Adam's physical characteristics can be used to argue he did not have two eyes, hair, and so forth.

desired result, the outcome is shame and recognition of one's loss of the proper use of sexuality. The Baalists became slaves of sexual desire, hardly the level of divine independence they sought.[30]

Thus J presents a powerful attack against the licentiousness of the fertility cults he confronted at the same time that he answers some of man's most perplexing questions about his origin. Given the horror with which Yahwism viewed the idolatry of Baalism, J can be excused if he allowed the God-given propriety of the sexual relationship to become sullied by its intimate association with man's disobedience. For his fellow Hebrews, sexuality was probably the most tempting route to disobedience of God's commandments, through the lure of the pagan fertility cults. By the time P wrote, of course, Baalism was no longer a problem: Yahwism had overcome its threat, and P could adopt his matter-of-fact, even optimistic, attitude toward the role of sex in human history.[31]

Coitus as Knowledge

A related matter that warrants consideration because of its importance in grasping the Old Testament view of human sexuality is the use of the word *know* to signify coitus (cf., e.g., Gen. 4:1). The Hebrew word *yadha* means much more than mere "intellectual comprehension"; it has the connotation of "experiencing," "becoming acquainted," even "being able." Today we might call such knowledge "existential" or substitute the word *experience* for it. For the Hebrew, "knowledge" was not simply "academic" but also very practical: "Knowledge of God" was not adherence to a body of abstract doctrines or principles, but experience of the reality of the Father of Abraham, Isaac, and Jacob, and devotion and obedience to him (cf. Hos. 4:1, 6; 6:3, 6). The choice of the word to denote sexual intercourse, then, has deep psychological overtones. It cannot be dismissed as merely a euphemism because such prudery would be out of keeping with the explicit frankness of the Old Testament with respect to so many other sexual matters. What then can be said of its use in this important sense?

30. John L. McKenzie, "The Literary Characteristics of Genesis 2—3," *Theological Studies*, 15 (1954), 571.
31. Cuthbert Simpson, "Genesis: Exegesis," *The Interpreter's Bible*, I (New York: Abingdon Press, 1952), 486, 510.

Given the Hebrew understanding of *yadha,* knowledge necessarily involved entering into relationship with that which is known. Hence, sexuality provides the opportunity for the most complete, most accurate, and most fulfilling knowledge of one another available to humans. And, within the context of our discussion of man's creation as male and female, an important aspect of sexual knowledge is the understanding of what it means to be a sexual being. One cannot really fully comprehend his maleness or her femaleness until it has been exercised in the deepest relationship possible with someone of the other sex. Thus the man's joyful response to the presentation of the woman ("This at last. . .," 2:23)—after the implicit rejection of the animals as "unfit" partners—indicates that for the first time he really knew what it meant to be a man. Coitus (as well as other heterosexual experience) conveys knowledge of who one is, in his or her most fundamental nature, as male or female. But at the same time it provides considerable knowledge of oneself to the other: Knower and known are inextricably interrelated, and in this relationship it is impossible not to convey some of oneself to the partner, the amount depending upon the nature of the relationship and the particular activity.

The Old Testament use of "know," therefore, reveals a psychological profundity perhaps unexpected from such a primitive source. In any attempt to reach a contemporary understanding of sexuality, it is important to keep in mind this recognition of the centrality of knowledge *of* as well as knowledge *about* with respect to sex.

2

Old Testament Development:
Hosea, The Song of Songs, and
Laws Regulating Sexual Conduct

Hosea: Marriage as an Image
for the Relationship Between God and Israel

One of the most striking and most important examples of the positive attitude in the Old Testament toward sexuality is the prophets' frequent use of marriage as an analogy for the relationship between Yahweh and his people. Deutero-Isaiah, for example, asserts that "your Maker is your husband, . . . the Lord has called you like a wife forsaken and grieved in spirit . . ." (54:5, 6; cf. 62:4–5); and Jeremiah proclaims that Yahweh remembers Israel's earlier "love as a bride" (2:2; cf. 3:8, 20). Ezekiel portrays in especially vivid language Yahweh's relationship to the faithless Israel as husband to wife: God reminds Israel how he spread his skirt over her nakedness, thus pledging his faith and entering into a covenant with her (16:8; cf. Ch. 23). The general consensus among scholars, however, rests with Hosea as the foremost expositor of this metaphor, and we shall look briefly at his use of it as illustrative of its many occurrences elsewhere.

Unfortunately, this task is complicated by the fact that there is a great deal of scholarly disagreement about the interpretation of the first three chapters of Hosea. This controversy results from the fact that the relationship of Hosea to Gomer, the "wife of harlotry," whom he takes at God's command, is far from clearly drawn, and numerous theories have arisen to explain it. For our purposes, however, James D. Smart's judgment is completely adequate: We can safely conclude that "Hosea seems to have been tragically unfortunate in his marriage, to have seen in it a human parable of God's relation with Israel, and to have acted out in relation to his wife a parable of God's redemptive love for Israel."[1] The actions of Hosea in Chapter 3 are thus symbols

1. "Hosea (Man and Book)," *IDB*, E–J, 650.

22

of God's past love for Israel, the forgiving and enduring nature of which Hosea vividly portrays in his unexpected action of ransoming the adulteress.

Hosea 1–3 is thus rich in theological concepts of central importance to the Old Testament faith, such as the nature of divine love and the idea of the covenant. Furthermore, in Chapter 11, Hosea introduces yet another of the great metaphors of the Judeo-Christian tradition, also one with sexual overtones: God is portrayed as Israel's patient and loving father, who calls his son out of Egypt, teaches him to walk, holds him in his arms, and feeds and comforts him in spite of his disobedience (vv. 1–4). As important as some of these ideas are, and as much as Hosea's images of God as husband and father can contribute to an understanding of Israel's history and religion, the details are of less interest to us than one simple fact: Yahweh's relationship to his chosen people could be seen and described as that of husband to wife or father to son, both of which are relationships with undeniably sexual elements.

The importance of this can hardly be overstressed as an illustration of the great value ascribed to sexuality by the Hebrews. Whatever the shortcomings in the practical realities of marriage in ancient Israel, the use by Hosea and other prophets of marriage and parenthood as symbols for God's relationship to Israel bespeaks a very high view of human sexuality. In keeping with this Hebrew stress on sexuality as central and good, and in light of the very personal nature of Hosea's use of the metaphor, one is led to conclude that for him the relationship of husband and wife was simply the best and most easily understood analogy of the relationship of Yahweh to Israel he could find. Thus, into the Judeo-Christian tradition entered one of its central images of its God, and it was a basically sexual one, i.e., God as husband. Later, however, the sexual nature of the image was either ignored totally, or lost through the excessive use of allegory.

Furthermore, it is important to note that Hosea's use of this imagery adds a unique element to the understanding of the man-woman relationship current in his time, namely, "an expression of sexuality in terms of genuine relationship." Moving beyond the dominative and therefore exploitative concept of marriage, Hosea saw the marriage relationship as analogous to the covenant between Yahweh and his people. Although *covenant* is a political term that can be interpreted

as an unequal treaty between the god and the people, it also has relational connotations in a deeply personal and emotional sense, as illustrated by the covenant of friendship between David and Jonathan (1
Sam. 20:8). And the characteristics of the divine covenant, Hosea
implied, must also apply to the one between husband and wife: "stead-
fast love, mutual compassion (suffering with the other), intimacy, and
ready response."[2]

Hosea of course did not reject totally the institutions he inherited—
e.g., divorce is the man's prerogative (2:2), and he *buys* his wife
back (3:1)—but what is noteworthy is that "to speak of the man-
woman relationship in terms of mutual response and self-giving, a life
of genuine sharing, a mutual discovery in each other, involved going
beyond the institutional pattern." This is seen most clearly in the fact
that Hosea broke the law which forbade taking back one's unfaithful
wife (Deut. 24:1–4) because of his commitment to her, despite the
pain and suffering he was caused. This indicates that God is willing
to break his own law to repair a broken relationship with him. As
Blenkinsopp concludes, there is a hint here "of the new relationship
which will rest not on obedience to law and the lawgiver but on the
sole impulse of the heart (Jer. 31:31–34)."[3] Such an attitude contributes a great deal to a contemporary understanding of what God
intends human sexuality and the male-female relationship to be, and
it goes a long way toward freeing us from the selfishly dominative and
exploitative models prevalent today.

The Song of Songs

Another illustration of the positive affirmation of sexuality in Old
Testament thought is the Song of Songs, surely the most explicitly
sexual book in the canon. In fact, probably no other book in the Bible
has provoked such differences of opinion and such a range of interpretations. This situation is no doubt attributable in part to the sexual
imagery used throughout the Song, but for the modern Christian
interpreter another problem arises: The book is not obviously "religious" at all, which has prompted a number of recent commentators
to speak of its "purely secular character."

Yet the title is a superlative, meaning "most beautiful song," and in
the dispute over its canonicity at the end of the first century A.D.,

2. Blenkinsopp, *Sexuality and the Christian Tradition*, pp. 36, 38.
3. *Ibid.*, p. 40.

Rabbi Akiba pronounced the judgment, "For all the world is not as worthy as the day on which the Song of Songs was given to Israel, for all the writings are holy, but the Song of Songs is the Holy of Holies."[4] Although the arguments concerning the various scholarly interpretations of the genesis and original meaning of the Song of Songs are interesting, it is beyond the scope of this inquiry to consider them.[5]

It is important to us, however, that the weight of current scholarship supports the view that the book is most clearly a loose collection of lyrics, with no theme other than love between the sexes, and no purpose other than praise of this love. There is no apparent intention to symbolize divine love and no evidence that pagan religious rites were the source of the lyrics, nor is there any moral to the book. Roland E. Murphy, e.g., cites with obvious approval the view of Gillis Gerlemann, who rules out a marriage context for the Song (even for 3:6–11) and "argues that we are dealing with love songs that simply extol love between the sexes."[6] Although the historical question of how such a book entered the canon is interesting,[7] more important to us is the information the Song of Songs conveys about the meaning of human sexuality and the Old Testament attitude toward it. On this topic, several things may be said.

The fact that the Song of Songs, which appears so secular to us, was preserved in a tradition in which religion pervaded every aspect of human existence provides a valuable insight into one element of Hebrew thought about sexuality. Interestingly, the reason for its

4. Quoted in N. K. Gottwald, "Song of Songs," *IDB*, R–Z, 421.

5. The following interpretations have gained the greatest support among scholars at various times: (1) as a drama, with two or three characters variously identified; (2) as an expurgated fertility-cult liturgy, originally celebrating the dying and rising of the god and his reunion with the mourning goddess; (3) as an allegory of the love of God for either Israel or the Church (or sometimes of Christ for the soul); and, (4) as a collection of pastoral lyrics, perhaps wedding songs, with no particular internal organization.

6. "Form-Critical Studies in the Song of Songs," *Interpretation*, XXVII (October, 1973), 416; hereafter cited as "Studies."

7. The scholarly consensus seems to be that canonicity was based primarily on the imputed Solomonic authorship, with a strictly secular interpretation prevalent before Jamnia. Indeed, as Gottwald suggests, the allegorical interpretation probably arose only after canonicity when the rabbis tended to look for esoteric religious meaning in a book that confronted them as already canonical. (See "Song of Songs," 422.) When the Christian Church decided its canon, the allegorical interpretation had been prevalent for some time and was easily adapted by replacing God and Israel with Christ and the Church. This assured the Song of Songs a place in the Christian canon despite its apparently secular, sensual content.

preservation seems to lie in this very fact of the inseparability of religion from the rest of life, especially in the Wisdom school in which
the Song was preserved. That is, the sages viewed the Song in the
light of the Wisdom literature which was gaining great importance in
the postexilic period, and hermeneutically this suggests, as pointed out
above, that "the primary meaning of the Song would then have to do
with human sexual love—the experience of it, its delights, its fidelity,
and its power."[8]

But for the sages, true to their Hebrew tradition, this does not mean
that the book was "secular." Indeed, this distinction would not even
have occurred to them, and the Song is secular only by our modern
definition, which makes a facile distinction alien to the mentality of
those who were responsible for the preservation of the Song. Although
God neither appears nor is mentioned in it (which makes it "secular"
for us), for the sages he is not absent from the Song, nor are his love
and concern for his creatures unmanifested in it. Rather they are
clearly shown in the enjoyment and pleasure (given by God to man
in the creation) which the lovers find in each other and in their sur-
roundings. Although this view may strike us as strange and somehow
"unchristian," it is a direct result of the presentations of creation in
Genesis and the later Hebrew development of the notion of God's
inseparability from and total involvement in his *good* creation, especially as manifested in the Wisdom school.

The Song of Songs was preserved in the tradition, then, precisely
because the sages did not distinguish between writings which explicitly
mention God (i.e., the "sacred") and those which do not (i.e., the
"secular"), even if the latter deal vividly and forthrightly with sexual
love. Since God created everything, everything spoke of his love for
his creatures if used as he intended. The Wisdom school was therefore concerned about, interested in, and approving of the relationship
between man and woman (including its attendant pleasures) as indications—perhaps one of the clearest indications—of God's love and
concern for man. The Song of Songs thus expresses the same wonder
as Proverbs 30:19 at "the way of a man with a maiden," and it illustrates the same affirmative view of sexual love as Proverbs 5:18–19:

> And rejoice in the wife of your youth,
> a lovely hind, a graceful doe.

8. Murphy, "Studies," 422.

> Let her affection fill you at all times with delight,
> be infatuated always with her love.

The allegorical interpretation of the Song, which must be rejected,[9] can nevertheless be instructive in this context. This view sees the love of the lover for the beloved as representative of God's love for man, which clearly was not the original intent or meaning of the poems we call the Song of Songs. But the allegorists may have been right in their conclusion—that the Song does indeed show God's love for man—although wrong in the way in which they thought this purpose was accomplished—through the symbol of earthly love as a representation of divine love. That is, we can safely assert that the Song does contain an allusion to God's love for man, *not* by way of direct analogy but in that God has given sexuality to man to enjoy, a loving gift from a loving Creator.

Such a view would be in keeping with one of the elements of the kerygma of the Wisdom school: that man is free and is trusted to enjoy the God-given gifts that are necessary for his existence. In Ecclesiastes 3:11, for instance, Qoheleth writes that God "has made everything beautiful in its time" (cf. vv. 1–9), and 2:24–25 illustrates well the point at hand:

> There is nothing better for a man than that he should eat and drink, and find enjoyment in his toil. This also, I saw, is from the hand of God; for apart from him who can eat or who can have enjoyment?[10]

To be included in this view is man's sexuality (cf. Proverbs 5:18–19; cited earlier), a gift from God meant to be enjoyed, though rationally and responsibly: After the admonition to "rejoice" in youth and to enjoy it, Qoheleth adds, "But know that for all these things God will

9. One may ask why I earlier readily accepted an allegorical interpretation of Hosea, whereas I dismiss such a reading of the Song of Songs. A helpful analogy can be found in efforts to solve the question of the relationship between the Old and New Testaments through the method of typological interpretation: To prevent excesses, the text itself must present the type-antitype relationship, at least implicitly. Similarly, the key here also seems to be that something in the text itself must suggest that an allegory is intended. In Hosea's case, this is clearly present (cf. 1:2); it is not in the Song of Songs. Thus there is the danger that an allegorical interpretation enables the interpreter to find in the book whatever his imagination desires.

10. Cf. 3:12–13: "I know that there is nothing better for [men] than to be happy and enjoy themselves as long as they live; also that it is God's gift to man that every one should eat and drink and take pleasure in all his toil." The emphasis is clearly on present earthly enjoyment (3:22), and the value and advantages of youth are recognized (11:9—12:7).

bring you into judgment" (11:9). The Song of Songs is a clear indication that the sages considered man's sexuality as a gift to be rejoiced in and enjoyed: Enjoyment is a gift of God, and man is ordained to enjoy sexual pleasures responsibly.

The preservation of the Song of Songs is therefore a symbol of Israel's positive valuation of marriage and sexual love. In fact, the Song is significant precisely in that it reminds us of a central fact of Yahwism too often overlooked today, namely, the goodness of *all* creation, including man's physical body and his sexual nature. In its vivid descriptions of the body of the beloved, the love and sexual passion of the lovers, and the beauty of the countryside, there is no question that the Song is stating unequivocally that these are all intended and therefore good parts of God's purpose in creation, to be celebrated and not denied.

Closely related to this point is the practical illustration provided by the Song of Songs of the Hebrew notion of psychophysical unity presented in the preceding chapter. This concept of psychophysical unity underlies the Song and gives it much of its power. Unlike most current thought on the subject, for the ancient Hebrew there was no split between love and passion. That is, love was not "spiritual," rendering the physical aspect relatively unimportant; rather, as the Song of Songs clearly shows, the more one loves, the more one's appreciation and enjoyment of the other's body increases. An important aspect of psychophysical unity is the inseparability of the body and the emotions, from which follows the close connection between sensuality and love: "In sex this unity between the emotions and the body reaches its highest degree, for the physical act becomes the emotional act par excellence."[11] This is a crucial concept to which we shall return in the final chapter.

Laws Governing Sexual Conduct

That the positive attitude toward human sexuality presented in the Genesis creation accounts was generally held in Israel is illustrated by the prophetic use of human sexual relationships as metaphors for divine-human relationships and by the composition and preservation in the Wisdom tradition of such a celebration of sexual love as the Song of Songs. There is no prudery in the Old Testament where sexual

11. Herold S. Stern, "The Concept of Chastity in Biblical Society," *Journal of Sex Research*, 2 (July, 1966), 93.

matters are concerned. Sexuality is seen as an important part of human life, inseparable from other facets of existence. Furthermore, the Hebrews realized the awesome power of sexuality, even if they did not consider it "sacred" in the sense in which Israel's neighbors thought it was.

Despite their generally positive attitude toward sex, therefore, the Hebrews were well aware, as mentioned previously, that even though God intended the creation for man's use and enjoyment, there are limits to the appropriate and responsible use of God's gifts. Thus, because of both the inescapable, central role of sexuality in life and the great potential for its misuse and abuse, a number of laws developed to regulate sexual behavior. A summary examination of some of these laws will facilitate our effort to understand the Old Testament attitude toward sexuality because the laws of ancient civilizations are among the most valuable artifacts we possess. By examining the regulations and sanctions which a society places upon its citizens, we can discover not only the polity of the society but also the beliefs and attitudes that underlie this structure and give it form.

Beyond any specific information that the Old Testament laws governing sexual conduct might convey, they clearly indicate the extreme seriousness of the Hebrew attitude toward sexuality. Nowhere, however, do these laws imply the condemnation of sex as such or the idea that it is evil in any way. Neither the prophets nor the laws put any special emphasis on sexual sin: Such sin is denounced not because it is *sexual* but because it is the vehicle for damaging one's relationship with one's fellows or with God. The concern of the law, then, is with the *uses* to which human sexuality is put, with the proper and fitting manifestations of its unavoidable power, and often in the context of *cultic* purity as opposed to *sexual* purity.

Indeed, as Louis M. Epstein points out, the pre-exilic Hebrews had to borrow their terminology for sexual morality, using words and concepts that denoted other kinds of sins as well, such as idolatry, violence, or even disgusting food. He concludes that originally Hebrew sexual morality was more concerned with morality and less with sex—sex was just not a "special problem in the pattern of social conduct," nor were sex offenses treated as if "they belonged to a special department of human psychology. They were sins like every other sin."[12]

12. *Sex Laws and Customs in Judaism* (New York: Bloch Publishing Co., 1948), pp. 4–5; hereafter cited as *Sex Laws.*

It is also important to stress once more the crucial significance to the Hebrews of procreation as a major purpose and goal of sex. Especially in the early period, when survival was at stake, the divine command/promise to Abraham influenced opinion on any sexual question.[13] In fact, it is probably safe to say that, in some sense, this two-fold concern about cultic purity and procreation (which cannot ultimately be separated) underlies *all* of the Old Testament laws about sexual behavior. It shows up most clearly, however, in several regulations at which we shall now look.

Sexual Organs

The surprising prohibition of a wife's seizing the "private parts" of a man with whom her husband is fighting (Deut. 25:11–12) indicates that the adversary male's reproductive power is more important than a wife's "natural" instinct to help her husband in any way she can. The importance of progeny to a man is so great that absolute priority is given to the protection of the organs that permit him to reproduce. This law may be related to another which excludes from the assembly of God anyone "whose testicles are crushed or whose male member is cut off" (Deut. 23:1), either of which the wife might do in attempting to rescue her husband.

S. R. Driver says that this exclusion, "in so far as it is not a protest against mutilation in the service of a heathen deity," is most likely based on a reason similar "to that referred to in 14:1: the deliberate mutilation of the nature which God has given to man is inconsistent with the character of Jehovah's people."[14] Thus the close link in

13. And of course the P source, written in exile, recognized and stressed that Israel had to "be fruitful and multiply" in order to survive.
14. *A Critical and Exegetical Commentary on Deuteronomy,* Vol. V of the International Critical Commentary (New York: Charles Scribner's Sons, 1916), p. 260. Deuteronomy 14:1 says, "You are the sons of the Lord your God; you shall not cut yourselves or make any baldness on your foreheads for the dead." Because, as we have seen, the proper use of sexuality was so important to Yahwism, for an action that destroys one's sexual capacity (i.e., castration) the penalty was apparently considerably more stringent than for other forms of mutilation, namely, exclusion from the "assembly of God," which was the entire community as it came together for different purposes, especially for worship. For the Hebrew, such exclusion was tantamount to death because individual identity was secondary to and dependent upon membership in the community. There was a great "fluidity of transition from the individual to the society and *vice versa*" since "the individual could not come into existence at all without some form of society, and depends upon it for his growth and development," and since "the society finds articulate expression only through the individuals who constitute it." For the

Hebrew thought between religion and sexuality (especially as manifest in the power of procreation) is again clearly demonstrated: Those who were sexually blemished were not acceptable to God (this "blemish" could even extend to the *way* in which an individual himself was procreated—cf. Deut. 23:2, which excludes bastards "even to the tenth generation").

Bestiality, Homosexuality, and "Seed-wasting"

The laws against bestiality (Exod. 22:19; Lev. 18:23; 20:15–16; Deut. 27:21) and homosexuality (Lev. 18:22; 20:13) appear to be based on three major concerns. First, such relations were simply unnatural. In the Hebrew view, moral law and natural law—both products of the one God—could not conflict. Thus "to defy nature's law is to violate the revealed law of morality. What nature abhors the law prohibits."[15] And in the judgment of the Israelites, nature clearly decreed that the human male should engage in sexual relations with the human female. Any deviation from this pattern—whether with another male or with an animal—was forbidden.

Second, and closely related, bestiality and homosexuality "wasted seed" that should be used to propagate descendants of Abraham and to fulfill Yahweh's command/blessing. Since procreation was impossible in both of these cases, the unnaturalness of the relations was compounded by their inability to result in the birth of offspring. Thus by human action, Yahweh's intention for sexuality was purposely thwarted.

Third, there is a link between these types of sexual misconduct and idolatry. The Canaanites frequently represented their gods in the form of animals,[16] and it is not unreasonable to assume that sexual

---

Hebrew, though, membership in the "corporate personality" of the society remained most crucial because Yahweh's "covenant was with the nation, not with the individual Israelites except as members or representatives of the nation." See H. Wheeler Robinson, *Corporate Personality in Ancient Israel*, Facet Books (Philadelphia: Fortress Press, 1964), pp. 6, 20, 26, and *passim*; hereafter cited as *Corporate Personality*.

15. Epstein, *Sex Laws*, p. 132.

16. Cf. Exodus 32, the story of the golden calf: When Moses is detained on Mount Sinai, the people call on Aaron to "make us gods, who shall go before us." Aaron agrees and makes a golden bull, a fertility symbol in many ancient religions; the people then proclaim, "These are your Gods, O Israel, who brought you up out of the land of Egypt," and they worship it. The response of Moses, prompted by Yahweh's wrath, has been immortalized by Cecil B. DeMille and Charlton Heston.

relations with beasts entered into some of their fertility rituals (cf. Lev. 18:23–30). Homosexuality, of course, was closely associated with pagan sexual practices, which featured male as well as female cult prostitutes (cf. Deut. 23:17: "There shall be no cult prostitute [*kadeshah*] of the daughters of Israel, neither shall there be a cult prostitute [*kadesh*] of the sons of Israel"). This law clearly considers homosexuality to be less a sexual offense than a manifestation of idolatry.

The story of Onan, frequently cited as a classic example of "seed-wasting," merits brief examination here. Onan was called upon to "perform the duty of a brother-in-law" for his dead brother Er, namely, to produce from Er's widow Tamar a male descendant who would perpetuate his name and gain his inheritance. "But Onan knew that the offspring would not be his; so when he went in to his brother's wife he spilled his semen on the ground, lest he should give offspring to his brother" (Gen. 38:9). For this sin, Yahweh killed him.

As is now generally acknowledged, Onan's sin was certainly not masturbation ("onanism"), but neither was it a mere "wasting of seed" as such: Onan's death was not the result of the *physical* act of wasting semen but rather of his refusal to perform the levirate duty to impregnate his brother's widow. That is, he was really guilty of consciously rejecting one of the most important religious duties of a brother. This story illustrates the elevation of sexuality by the Hebrews to the sphere of *personal* relationships rather than mere animalistic, magical functions: Onan's sin was not the "wasting of seed" per se but rather his failure to fulfill a *religious* duty (which was manifested through sex) and thus his failure to meet the *relational* demands of his covenant with Yahweh and with his brother. We see here another element of the Old Testament's humanization and personalization of sexuality that is also illustrated by Hosea's covenantal emphasis.

Adultery

Regarding adultery, the concern about procreation comes to the fore, although there was a metaphorical equation in Hebrew thought of idolatry with harlotry and adultery, which indicates that considerations of religious purity also enter in.[17] The primary interest of the law itself appears to be maintenance of the male's control over the

17. See, e.g., Ezek. 16 and 23; Jer. 3:1–10 and 5:7–9; and Mal. 2:11. Cf. also Exod. 34:16; Deut. 31:16; and Judges 2:16–17.

purity of his bloodline.[18]   The Old Testament makes fairly clear both in the laws and in descriptions of marriages that the woman was, in a fundamental sense, the property of her husband; the very word for "husband" in Hebrew—*baal*—originally meant "lord" or "proprietor" (and is of course the same term used for the local deities). Coitus with another man, therefore, was fundamentally an affront to the husband's exclusive possession of his wife, especially since it rendered impossible determination of the paternity of the children she bore.

This "chattel motif" naturally led to a double standard, by which the wife could sin only against her own marriage whereas the husband could not sin against his marriage but only against that of another man.   The husband's right to exclusive possession of his wife, which was violated by *her* adultery, was then clearly a non-reciprocal right: If the woman were "unattached," no harm was done (except perhaps to the pride of her father or brothers);[19] but if she were married and thus the "repository" for her husband's seed, the law dealt harshly with both parties.[20]

Nevertheless, as Epstein maintains, the biblical law on adultery went a significant step beyond other ancient laws in considering adultery to be a moral crime as well as a personal injury to the husband.[21]   Again, we see the beginnings of an emphasis upon the *relationship* and mutuality of the partners—*both* of whom are equally bound by a suprapersonal law—rather than upon the exclusive proprietary rights of only one party.   No longer can the husband in his passion seek immediate revenge in a fit of jealousy according to the ancient rules of the tribal feud.   Rather he must present his case to the appropriate officers of the law *for them* to prosecute as the law prescribes.   In this in-

18. The determination of paternity was crucial because of the Hebrew concept of corporate personality: The living group was extended into the future as part of its unity, and hence there arose "the dominant aspiration of the Hebrew to have male children to perpetuate his name, the name that was so much part of himself that something of him died when his name ceased." See Robinson, *Corporate Personality*, p. 4.

19. See, e.g., Exod. 22:16–17; Deut. 22:28–29; and the story of the revenge of the rape of Dinah, Gen. 34, esp. v. 31.

20. See, e.g., Lev. 20:10; Deut. 22:22–27; and the ordeal concerning the "tokens of virginity," Deut. 22:13–21.

21. *Sex Laws*, p. 199.   That is—despite several primitive incidents reported in the Old Testament but not accepted as standards by the law—in the eyes of the law the crime and penalty remain the same whether the husband prosecutes or forgives or the guilty male offers to pay a ransom; it is no longer a matter between the guilty couple and the *husband* but between them and the *law*.

stance, the Old Testament law on adultery made an admirable advance toward fulfilling the purpose of law as defined by Epstein: namely, "to supersede primitive tribal usages and to regulate human affairs by standards of equity rather than of passion. . . for the purpose of maintaining order and decency in human affairs."[22]

Military Deferment

Even with its emphasis on procreation and cultic purity, it is important to note that the Old Testament recognizes other aspects of sexuality in its laws. One of the most important of these is seen in the law allowing a newly wedded male one year at home before he has to serve with the army (Deut. 24:5; cf. 20:7). Again, there is no question that a central concern here is that the man have a chance to produce progeny before risking his life in battle and perhaps to be at home long enough to assure that the child is his. Nevertheless, the wording of the law—he is to be free for a year in order "to be *happy* with his wife"—indicates more than mere procreation. Certainly having a child was a source of joy for the Hebrew, but the particular wording seems to imply a concern for the importance of a good family life and for the sexual pleasures of the male-female relationship beyond procreation (an idea, as we have seen with respect to the Song of Songs, that was far from alien to the Hebrew mentality).

Circumcision

One further Old Testament law—circumcision—merits attention as an especially clear example of the close relationship between religion and sexuality in Hebrew life since it bears on the question of both procreation and cultic purity. In Genesis 17, Yahweh makes his covenant with Abraham to be kept forever: "Every male among you shall be circumcised. . ., and it shall be a sign of the covenant between me and you" (vv. 10–11). There are numerous theories as to the origin of circumcision among ancient peoples which range from reasons of hygiene, through puberty rites, to substitution for human sacrifice or proof of submission to God;[23] but the question of beginnings is not

22. *Ibid.*, p. 196.

23. Cf. Exod. 4:24–26 for possible support for these last two views. A concise summary of some of the more important of these theories is given in Charles Weiss, "Motives for Male Circumcision among Preliterate and Literate People," *Journal of Sex Research*, 2 (July, 1966), 76–84; hereafter cited as "Motives for Male Circumcision."

our concern. Whatever its origin, the meaning of circumcision for Old Testament religion is clear: It marks the individual as a participant in the Covenant, and its absence excludes him (cf. Exod. 12:48) even to the extent of rendering him contemptible (cf. 1 Sam. 14:6; 31:4).

Once again, a sexual symbol is used to denote the most important relationship of all, that of an individual to God. Every male descendant of Abraham thus bears the external proof of his membership in that covenant. As Theodor Gaster aptly puts it, "the Jew . . . carries in his flesh a constant reminder of the fact that his own self-perpetuation is also the perpetuation of Israel's mission and that the offspring which he begets are not merely his own heirs but also the prospective agents and witnesses of an eternal God."[24] There is good reason to believe, therefore, that this mark of Hebrew identity did not come about accidentally and merely happen to be placed on the particular part of the body that it was. Rather this organ was purposely chosen to carry the identifying sign of God's chosen people because it played such an essential role in furthering God's purpose for that people.

On the *sexual* organ of the male, then, is placed the symbol of his *religious* identity. Such identity is not gained, however, through the use of this organ in imitation of or participation in similar divine actions; rather circumcision, though undeniably sexual, indicates a nonsexual religious and moral commitment. That this is so is evident in the frequently used metaphor of "circumcision of the heart" (Deut. 30:6; 10:16; Jer. 4:4; cf. 6:10; 9:25), a figure which obviously means religious purity, goodness, and holiness. This image again shows the ease with which Hebrew thought associated religion and sexuality in profound religious statements, and once more we see that the Old Testament could use *sexual* imagery to make some of its most powerful *religious* points.

Conclusion

The portions of the Old Testament considered in this chapter—the prophetic images of God as husband and father, the explicit poetry of

24. *The Holy and the Profane* (New York: W. Sloane Associates, 1955), no page cited, quoted in Weiss, "Motives for Male Circumcision," p. 83. The concept of "corporate personality"—the easy transition from the identity and concerns of the individual to those of the society and vice versa—is clearly evident here.

the Song of Songs, and the various laws governing sexual conduct—
illustrate the prevalent attitude toward sexuality in Israel that we discovered in our examination of the Genesis creation accounts. Each in
its own way demonstrates the close link between religion and sexuality
in the Old Testament, the central role played by sex in Hebrew life
and thought, and the positive, healthy view of sex held in ancient
Israel. Although we have seen an emphasis placed on procreation and
cultic purity, it is clear that the Old Testament recognizes other elements of the relationship between male and female and considers
them as equally valid facets of this important gift of God to humanity.
For the Christian, it is of course necessary to ask how these ideas were
applied and developed in the New Testament; and with the background we have now gained of the Old Testament attitude toward
sexuality, we can examine the teachings on this topic of the two
dominant New Testament figures.

3

New Testament Development:
Jesus

After the abundance of statements in the Old Testament about the nature and purpose of human sexuality, it may be somewhat surprising to discover that the New Testament is relatively silent on the topic. If, as this book contends, sexuality is a fundamental aspect of human existence, one may well wonder why the central figures of the New Testament, together with those who endeavored to record their words and actions, did not have more to say on the subject. Since Christianity purports to be based on the teachings of Jesus of Nazareth, the Christian is considerably handicapped in this particular area by the paucity of statements about sex attributed to Jesus. Even Paul, who has gained an undeserved notoriety for his views on sex, actually said relatively little about it (although what he did say was pregnant with meaning, though ripe for misunderstanding).

As we examine some of the central New Testament statements about human sexuality, one reason for this puzzling lack of attention will become apparent: The New Testament is in organic continuity with the Old, and many scholars feel that where the New Testament actors or authors were basically satisfied with what the Old Testament taught, they did not bother to elaborate on that particular topic. This, of course, cannot be the sole explanation for the New Testament's relative silence;[1] in fact, if that were the case, the Christian would find little reason for going beyond the Old Testament for his understanding of human sexuality. Since a fundamental conviction of Christianity is that the New Covenant is indeed new and that Jesus did move con-

---

1. There were obviously both theological and historical reasons beyond the one mentioned in the text; but what is important to us is the recognition that much of what the Old Testament said about sexuality (which has been presented in the preceding two chapters) would have been accepted and assumed by the actors and authors of the New Testament.

siderably beyond the Judaism of his heritage, we must examine those insights that the New Testament does offer about the meaning of human sexuality, with an eye to both the similarities and the differences between the two Testaments.

Jesus' Appeal to God's Primordial Will

The continuity between the Old and New Testaments suggests a general point that needs to be mentioned before we turn to Jesus' statements that refer to sexuality. Jesus clearly asserted his adherence to the sacred writings of his fathers; this fact is most explicitly stated in Matthew 5:17: "Think not that I have come to abolish the law and the prophets; I have come not to abolish them but to fulfill them." A great deal has been written on the meaning of "fulfill" in this passage— and even more on Jesus' attitude toward the Jewish law—but the overwhelming consensus is that he did not reject the law but reaffirmed it, although in a way which in fact transformed it because of the authority he claimed. Even in his most scathing attack on the scribes and Pharisees, Jesus condemned only their *failure* to live up to the law, and he urged his followers to "practice and observe whatever they tell you," i.e., the law (Mt. 23:3).

Indeed, the emphasis throughout Matthew (as well as the rest of the Gospels) is on opposition to the rabbinic *interpretation* of the law, not to the law itself.[2] Whatever the precise theological meaning of "fulfill," then, the basic point of interest to us is clear: Jesus saw as his task not to bring a new law to replace the old one but rather to establish, to bring to full validity, the requirements of the law of Moses. He was to do this by revealing God's will (which the Torah contained) in its original sense and by clarifying doubtful points with the authority of the original giver of the law. This meant that he might even restate the law if necessary.

In fact, it is extremely important to note that Jesus thought that he was inaugurating God's earthly reign (see Mk. 1:15). Because the hour of salvation had come, Jesus' ethical demands, however similar in content to those of other moral teachers of antiquity, took on a unique note which Jesus expressed by repeatedly appealing to God's

2. Gerhard Barth, "Matthew's Understanding of the Law," in *Tradition and Interpretation in Matthew*, Percy Scott, trans. (Philadelphia: Westminster Press, 1963), p. 159.

primordial will as originally intended in creation. Since God was once more establishing his absolute reign, Jesus could present his message without concern for the circumstances of the "fallen" world and he could consider God's commandments completely free from the compromises of earthly life.[3] In the New Testament, then, religion and morality are inseparable because Jesus brought first and foremost a religious message—that in his ministry, the Kingdom of God was at hand—from which his moral demands arose.[4]

This union between religion and morality enabled Jesus to make a subtle but revolutionary shift in the thought of his day (and still so today): No longer was God's will done by inordinate attention to minor precepts with consequent neglect of the "weightier matters of the law, justice and mercy and faith" (which ought to be done *along with* the other, Mt. 23:23). The legalistic observance of every external "jot and tittle" championed by the Pharisees was no longer sufficient; rather, one's righteousness must *exceed* that of the scribes and Pharisees (Mt. 5:20). And this "extra measure" was to be gained not through better ritual and cultic observance but through the proper orientation of the heart, the right inner disposition—that of obedience to God's will, manifested externally through love of neighbor.

Indeed, according to Schnackenburg, Jesus relaid the foundation of ethics as such by making the moral value of an act dependent on the inner motivation of the heart. The external act is of course important, but only insofar as it is the fruit of the internal disposition (cf. Lk. 6:45; also Mt. 15:17–20). On the other hand, though, religious piety is empty without moral authentication through action.[5] I do not claim that this inseparability of religion and morality—manifesting itself in an appeal to God's original will in creation and an emphasis on inner motivation—is sufficient to explain the uniqueness and profundity of Jesus' teaching. Nevertheless, the union of religion and morality is of central importance in our effort to understand Jesus' statements that

3. Rudolf Schnackenburg, *The Moral Teaching of the New Testament*, J. Holland-Smith and W. J. O'Hara, trans. (New York: Herder & Herder, 1965), pp. 76, 80; hereafter cited as *Moral Teaching*. For Jesus, God's original purpose in creation was of course to be discovered primarily in the Jewish Scriptures—our Old Testament—though he frequently appealed to the order of nature observable around him (e.g., Mk. 4:3–20, 26–32; Mt. 5:44–45; 6:25–33).
4. Schnackenburg, *Moral Teaching*, pp. 13–16.
5. *Ibid.*, pp. 62, 67–70.

pertain to sexuality, and several of these statements are virtually unintelligible on any other hermeneutical principle.

For Jesus, then, although the law expresses the will of God, the two cannot be simply equated. The law serves the will of God, which is superior to the law *as its goal.*[6] This is the idea that Jesus expressed by returning to God's original will in creation in disputes over the law: The standard against which any question of *human* interpretation of the law must be judged is the *divine* purpose in promulgating the law. As W. D. Davies puts it, Jesus understood " the law in terms of the will of God, not the will of God in terms of the law," which seems to have been the Pharisees' problem.[7] Christian theology asserts that the work of Christ consisted in carrying through, fulfilling, the will of God. That Jesus so understood his mission is shown by the antitheses of the Sermon on the Mount: "You have heard that it was said . . . but I say to you . . . ." Thus the Christian must listen carefully whenever Jesus claims to be stating God's true will for man.

It is appropriate to add here that in this chapter Jesus' appeals to God's original intention in creation are being used in a purely *descriptive* sense, as a foundation for our later effort to construct a theological statement of human sexuality. Thus I am not concerned with determining their *normative* value or their application, as, for instance, with respect to the question of divorce today. It seems clear, however, that when we do consider these questions, we must be constantly aware that we still live in the "fallen" times, after Jesus' preaching but *before* his *parousia,* and not in the time of the original creation.

Jesus' Teachings on Marriage and Divorce

The relevance of the foregoing discussion to our concerns becomes apparent when we consider Jesus' teachings about marriage and divorce, which are the prime sources for discerning his understanding of human sexuality. In Mark 10:2–9[8] (cf. Mt. 19:3–9), the Pharisees try to trap Jesus by asking him about the perennial problem of divorce.

6. G. Barth, "Matthew's Understanding of the Law," p. 148.
7. "Law in the NT," *IDB,* K–Q, 97.
8. Vv. 10–12 are omitted here because the evidence indicates that they were not part of Jesus' original teaching. Mark often uses "private sessions" with the disciples as opportunities to present the early Church's interpretations of Jesus' teachings (cf., e.g., 4:10–34, esp. 33–34; 13:3–37). Internal support for this view is found in v. 11—the man is said to commit adultery "against" his wife, but, as we saw, in Jewish law a man could commit adultery only against the

Elsewhere Jesus is not hesitant to talk explicitly about this issue, but here he really addresses the more fundamental question of the nature of marriage, of the man-woman relationship, and thus, in a sense, of human sexuality. His questioners, perhaps aware of his strict views on the subject, want to force him to contradict the Mosaic law (and, in the Matthean version, to offend one side or the other in the rabbinic debate then raging over the *grounds* for divorce—cf. the addition of "for any cause").

At first it appears they may succeed when Jesus himself asks that the position of Moses be made clear. But then he uses the devastating tactic discussed above of referring to God's primordial will: He goes *behind* the law of Moses, which was really a "concession" to the selfishness of man in his "fallen" state; and he appeals to God's original intention in creation, adding insult to injury by quoting Scripture to prove his point. Whatever the current situation, Jesus says, God *created* man male and female so that they could come together in marriage, a physical union in which "they are no longer two but one flesh." This Semitic idiom is based on the concept of psychophysical unity discussed in Chapter 1 and indicates a merger of two complete personalities, not just two physical bodies. And this indissoluble "oneness," since it is God's intention, is not to be destroyed by man.

Although there is not enough evidence to allow us to determine exactly what Jesus had in mind in his interpretation of the "one-flesh" doctrine of Genesis, it is clear that he took it quite literally (cf. his forbidding of remarriage). Whatever the processes involved might be—whatever might happen "ontologically" or "mystically"—Jesus apparently thought that some kind of *real* union occurs in the marriage (and subsequent physical intercourse of a man and a woman), a bond that could not be eliminated merely by drawing up a "certificate of divorce," even if Moses had allowed this. In God's *original* purpose for man, according to Jesus, the union was to be permanent; and only because of man's disobedience and disordered relationships was this not the case. Hence, Jesus, with his keen insight into human nature and God's will for man, stated clearly what that will was "from the

---

husband of his partner; and in v. 12—the ability of the wife to divorce her husband assumed here suggests a Gentile audience since the practice was exceedingly rare in first-century Judaism. These three verses, then, are probably a later interpolation to bring the teaching into line with the practice of the Gentiles for whom this Gospel was written.

beginning of creation" with respect to the purpose of marriage and the man-woman relationship, surely of great importance to us as we undertake to present a contemporary Christian understanding of human sexuality.

Given this view of the nature of marriage, Jesus took a rather strict position concerning divorce and remarriage. Since God's will was that the one-flesh union be indissoluble, divorce was, in the deepest sense, literally impossible, and remarriage therefore necessarily constituted adultery (Lk. 16:18; Mt. 5:32; 19:9). It is important to note that in the antithetical presentation of this teaching in Matthew 5:31–32, Jesus is again implicitly appealing to God's original purpose for man. As we would expect, he is not denying any of the provisions of the law but rather giving them their ultimate meaning, bringing them in line with the primordial will of God which they were supposed to support in the first place. This can hardly be interpreted as *rejecting* the law; rather, it is upholding the law by bringing it into accord with the purpose for which it was given. And it is clear that in Jesus' view God intended marriage to be a permanent union which possesses a value quite apart from that attributed to it by its human participants, a value which in God's eyes precludes its arbitrary dissolution by human action. Jesus' prohibition of divorce and remarriage therefore implies a very high view of sexual union between husband and wife.

Finally, it is significant that Jesus appears to stress the unitive, relational aspect of marriage more than the procreative, again in contrast to the practice of his society. Although he had a warm affection for children and clearly valued a strong family, his citation of Genesis 2:24 as the "definition" of marriage and his prohibition of divorce (one of the major reasons for which was the alleged barrenness of the wife) and remarriage certainly emphasize the companionship side of the relationship (I have found no evidence that the "one flesh" was interpreted as referring to a child born of the merely sexual union of the "two").

Jesus' Attitude Toward Women

One of the most significant implications of the life and ministry of Jesus for a contemporary understanding of human sexuality receives, strangely perhaps, no explicit support in his teachings; it is implicit, however, not only in his statements about marriage and divorce but also in many other places. There is little question that in a culture in which women held a subordinate, subservient place,[9] Jesus must have stood out for his radical attitude toward them.

By asserting the "one-flesh" indissolubility of marriage, Jesus protected the place of women in the relationship of the sexes. No longer could the husband treat his wife as mere chattel, a possession to be put away if he found "some indecency" in her, interpreted in Jesus' time to mean even burning the bread. If the man and woman truly became one flesh according to God's will, a mutual relationship and obligation were implied that substantially changed the current attitude toward women. A woman could not be seen merely as a sexual being provided for her husband's pleasure and for bearing children (preferably male), nor could she be easily divorced if she failed in either of these duties.

For Jesus a woman was a person, a human being, an individual of equal worth with men before God; and she was to be treated accordingly. Conspicuous by its absence in this context is *any* reference by Jesus to the submission of women to their husbands which is so prevalent in many other New Testament writings and in the culture of his time (cf. 1 Cor. 11:3; 14:34–35; Eph. 5:22–24; Col. 3:18; 1 Tim. 2:11–14; and 1 Pet. 3:1–6). Apparently he was more concerned with the equal dignity and honor of the sexes than with the maintenance of the subordination he observed.

Thus Jesus did not hesitate to speak to women (in disregard of his community's rules—cf. Jn. 4:27: His disciples "marveled that he was talking with a woman")[10] and to heal them—including, among others,

9. For a concise summary of the low status of woman in rabbinic Judaism, see Albrecht Oepke, "γυνή," *Theological Dictionary of the New Testament*, I, Gerhard Kittel, ed., Geoffrey W. Bromiley, trans. (Grand Rapids: Eerdmans Publishing Company, 1964), 781–82.

10. I am well aware of the many problems attendant upon the use of the discourses of the Fourth Gospel as illustrative of Jesus' actual words and actions; and I am not claiming any greater authenticity for them than biblical scholars are willing to recognize. Nevertheless, even if John's depictions of Jesus are once removed from a "historical" account, he does present one interpretation of Jesus that was current and apparently accepted in the earliest tradition. Furthermore, there is nothing in John's accounts with respect to our particular interests that *contradicts* the picture of Jesus presented in the Synoptics. For these reasons, I think that it is acceptable to utilize whatever information John can add to the limited presentation in the Synoptics of Jesus' views about human sexuality, bearing in mind constantly that John's accounts are more interpretive and theologically oriented than are those of the other evangelists.

Mary Magdalene, Peter's mother-in-law, the daughter of the Syro-Phoenician woman, and the woman bent over for eighteen years. The last instance is especially significant because he risked the wrath of the Pharisees by breaking the Sabbath rule to heal this *woman*. Jesus' positive attitude toward women is also shown by his willingness to have women listen to his teaching and learn from him about spiritual matters: He delivered some of his deepest theological insights to the Samaritan woman at the well (Jn. 4:7–30)—a woman who, not insignificantly, was furthermore guilty of specifically sexual sins—and Mary is commended for preferring to listen to Jesus' teaching rather than join Martha in the "woman's work" of serving a meal (Lk. 10:38–42).

The Absence of Women Disciples

A frequently asked question today is, "If Jesus thought so highly of women, why were there no women disciples?" A detailed examination of this question is beyond the scope of this book, but several comments are in order. The question is usually asked with reference to the twelve apostles, who are generally thought to have been Jesus' intimate associates. But Hans Conzelmann points out that there is a distinction between the Twelve and the apostles, who were equated only later. Furthermore, the historical role of the Twelve is not at all clear, nor are even their names. Literary-critical analysis helps to explain this unusual situation: The Twelve are not mentioned in many older pieces of the tradition and make their appearance only when these separate pieces were combined into longer narratives. In addition, there was not even a clear definition of "apostle" for some time.[11]

The importance of this lack of clarity about the Twelve for our concerns lies in the fact that it leads to the assumption that the apostles came together for the first time only upon Jesus' death. Thus Conzelmann suggests that the notion of the "Twelve apostles" is a post-resurrection phenomenon designed to fulfill the Jewish-Christian desire to tie Jesus into the history of Israel; the Twelve then would represent the twelve tribes of the people of Israel, an interpretation supported by the fact that, though they were mostly Galileans, they chose to live in Jerusalem.[12] This suggested genesis of the idea of the

11. *History of Primitive Christianity*, John E. Steely, trans. (Nashville: Abingdon Press, 1973), pp. 55, 148, 41.
12. *Ibid.*, pp. 39–40.

Twelve, together with the androcentric nature of Judaism, provides a plausible explanation of why women are not mentioned among the "intimate circle" of Jesus' apostles.

With this information before us, however, a more positive response can be made. Put quite simply, there *were* women disciples, as the Gospels make clear. Luke reports that women accompanied Jesus and his male disciples on their itinerant ministry and in fact even supported their work financially (8:2–3). Furthermore, Jesus had close friends who were women (cf., e.g., Jn. 11:5). It is also important in this regard that women were the ones who remained at the foot of the cross, were the first witnesses to the resurrection, and were present in the upper room with the remaining male disciples. In short, with respect to matters of the faith, Jesus clearly considered women to be as important as men, and their absence from the Twelve is no indication that he did not accord them a high place in his thought.

In light of the situation at the time when Jesus lived, these examples clearly indicate that no explicit statements by Jesus are necessary to show how seriously he held the belief that women were worthy of his love and concern. It is true, of course, that Jesus' purpose was not to bring about social equality but to inaugurate God's kingdom. In doing this without regard to the sex of the individual, however, he left a legacy that should have had considerable positive influence on the place of woman in Christian thought. Our task, though, is to present what Jesus' teachings reveal about the *nature* of the male-female relationship.

Something of this has been indicated above with respect to Jesus' assertion of the one-flesh indissolubility of marriage, and one further comment will serve well to relate this section to an important theological theme of our study. Despite the low social and cultic status of women in his time, Jesus addressed them as equals before God, i.e., as they were *meant to be* originally by God in creation and are meant to be ultimately in redemption. Before the Fall, before man's relationships with God and other humans were disordered, woman was not subordinate and subservient, and the sexual relationship had a considerably different tone.

Christian faith affirms that Jesus Christ is the New Adam (Rom. 5; cf. 1 Cor. 15:20–22) and that anyone who believes in him is "a new creation" (2 Cor. 5:17). In this role, Christ serves as God's agent in reconciling all humans—male and female—to himself and thus to each other. He reverses and corrects precisely what happened in the Garden and overcomes the disruption of the relationship between God and the man and woman and the consequent disordering of their own relationship. Just as male and female were one in creation and enjoyed a communion and mutual sharing later obscured by their disobedience, so Christ offers the opportunity for that communion to be regained in redemption. Christ, the agent of creation (1 Cor. 8:6; Col. 1:15–20; Heb. 1:2), is also the agent of redemption; and in redemption he restores the original intent of God in creation.

Jesus' Teachings on Adultery

Jesus' view of the equality of the sexes and his compassionate treatment of women receive practical illustration in a story that introduces us to another area of his teaching which is important to our study. In the story of the adulterous woman (Jn. 8:1–11), Jesus makes clear that the penalty is not to be inflicted on the woman alone (as, indeed, would have been contrary to the law the Pharisees themselves cited—cf. Lev. 20:10). Furthermore, he indicates to her accusers that her sin, though sexual in nature and against God's purpose for marriage, was no worse and thus no more deserving of punishment than their more subtle sins of pride and hypocrisy. Indeed, Jesus consistently considered the harlots' sexual sins to be less grievous than the Pharisees' "spiritual sins" (cf. Mt. 21:31), probably because he learned early that the former were, not surprisingly, much more open to his message than those who were convinced they held the truth already.

Jesus' most famous teaching on adultery, Matthew 5:27–28—"You have heard that it was said, 'You shall not commit adultery.' But I say to you that every one who looks at a woman lustfully has already committed adultery with her in his heart"—shows these same concerns: What really matters, Jesus hyperbolically states, is one's inner motivation, whether actualized in an external act or not. In lust, as in adultery, the *created purpose* of sex—to enable a man and a woman to unite in the most intimate of relationships—cannot be fulfilled, and the object of lust remains just that, i.e., an object to be used to gain the self's own satisfaction without regard for the other's needs. Jesus thus implicitly denies the use of a woman (or a man) as a mere "sex object" at the same time that he stresses once again God's original will for sexuality. Since in lustful desire as such, the *physical* act is not yet committed, the decisive factor is the will or intention. Clearly for Jesus, sex is much more than the physical merging of bodies if the mere wrong desire is as open to condemnation as the wrong act.

It should be noted that, given his positive view of sexuality argued earlier, Jesus surely was not condemning the natural, involuntary, transitory sexual impulse, a perfectly proper aspect of human sexuality as created by God. His concern was rather twofold: first, that one not deliberately keep oneself in a prolonged state of desire for another that represents the actual wish or intent to commit the act, deterred only by lack of opportunity; and second, that the object of one's sexual impulses be appropriate—this is shown by the use of the phrase "commit adultery," which implies that the "woman" mentioned is *not* a legitimate partner. There is certainly no condemnation of proper sexual expression. It is hard to believe that these two verses could have been understood so often as indicating an anti-sex bias on Jesus' part and encouraging celibacy, but such are the vagaries of biblical interpretation.

Jesus' Attitude Toward the Family

Biblically speaking, the family may be seen as both the proper context for and the result of the sexual relationship, and Jesus' positive regard for the family has been implicit throughout his teachings on marriage, divorce, and adultery. In addition, his attitude is illustrated by his extraordinary fondness for children, whom he specifically blessed as models for entrance into the Kingdom (Mk. 10:13–16; Mt. 18:1–4; 19:13–15; Lk. 18:15–17) and whom he frequently healed (e.g., Mk. 5:35–43; 7:24–30; 9:14–29; and many others); by his concern about his mother and provision for her care even in the agony of his final suffering on the cross (Jn. 19:26–27); and by his special understanding of the father-son relationship together with his application of it to God (e.g., Jn. 5:17–18).[13]

On the other hand, there are also a number of sayings of Jesus which we must examine because they appear to degrade and even threaten

13. John's point in the two instances cited may, of course, have been more theological than historical; nevertheless, his use of these particular examples indicates the importance attached to family relationships by the early Church as well as by John himself, who is one of the canonical commentators on the life of Jesus. John must have felt that it would not be out of keeping with Jesus' attitude for him to use such relationships to make theological points.

the family and its relationships. We shall consider one fairly commonly accepted explanation in light of which most of the sayings can be understood. One of the sayings, however, requires slightly more detailed examination because of the role it has played in traditional Christian interpretations of sex.

Among the sayings which can be dismissed with a brief common explanation are those statements in which Jesus appears to deny his own family (Mt. 12:46–50) and demands that his hearers "hate" and forsake their various relatives (e.g., Lk. 9:59–62; 14:25–27; Mt. 10:34–39). There is considerable agreement among scholars of assorted theological leanings and professional specializations that the central theme of Jesus' preaching was the coming of the Kingdom of God (cf. the first words of his public ministry, Mk. 1:15, as well as Mt. 6:33), one of the major features of which was the absolute supremacy of its claims upon the believer (cf. the parables of the Kingdom as "treasure in a field" and a "pearl of great value," which the finders will sell all they have in order to obtain, Mt. 13:44–45).

A careful examination of the passages under consideration indicates quite clearly that Jesus is *not* advocating the denial of family ties or the natural relationships of life, nor is he saying that in order to follow him one *must* cease to feel natural affection for relatives. He is simply saying that *if* conflicts arise (as he realized were likely), the demands of the Kingdom must come first—if natural affections war against God's will, they must be sacrificed for the Kingdom's sake. This interpretation is supported by the inclusion of the phrase, "yes, and even his own life," after the enumeration of all the relatives one must "hate" (Lk. 14:26), which puts the whole saying in the broader context of Jesus' ongoing theme of "losing one's life in order to find his life." However one interprets that cryptic saying, it certainly applies literally to very few.

In these hard sayings, then, Jesus is not disparaging the family and, thus, by implication, the sexual relationship. He is, rather, setting *priorities* that must be observed by those who follow him: If need be, everything must be given up for the Kingdom, even family ties, and one must recognize the Kingdom's greater claim that only those who do God's will are the true relatives of Christ. Indeed, far from demeaning the family, Jesus implicitly acknowledges the high regard he held for the mutual affections of the family by using family relationships in these examples of God's absolute claim upon us: He says in effect that when God demands it of us, *even* family ties—*even* those bonds of affection that should be dearest and most meaningful to us and the strongest on earth—have to be set aside. This is the *ultimate* sacrifice for the Kingdom, on a par with giving up one's very life.

One further saying of Jesus that has had an especially prominent influence on the Church's attitude toward sex can be interpreted in this same light, but because of its importance a slightly more detailed examination is necessary. In Matthew 19:10-12,[14] Jesus utters his unique words about those "who have made themselves eunuchs for the sake of the kingdom of heaven" after he mentions "eunuchs who have been so from birth" and "who have been made eunuchs by men," both of which were current rabbinical classifications. Except perhaps for Origen and other isolated cases, New Testament interpreters generally agree that Jesus' usage is figurative, but here the agreement ends: The interpretations of the meaning of the passage as a whole are legion.

Traditionally, this saying has been taken to refer to voluntary celibacy, to be undertaken only by those who are "able to receive this," which implies that this is a "higher way" of discipleship and thus indicates a basically anti-sexual bias on Jesus' part. However popular this view has been, the evidence against it is overwhelming. In the first place, there are *no* other statements or actions anywhere attributed to Jesus which suggest that he held such a view of sex. Furthermore, as we saw in Chapter 2, eunuchs held a very low place in Jewish thought, being "cut off" from religious communion and thus effectively "dead" (cf. Deut. 23:1). It is therefore not likely that Jesus would have set them up as models for the few "to whom it is given" to be able to do God's will fully.

Finally, and perhaps most important, is the context of the passage itself. It occurs between two affirmations of the *positive* nature of marriage and sexual relationships: Verses 3-9 present marriage as ordained by God in his original purpose and intention in creation; and verses 13-15 portray children, the fruit of marital sexual activity, as

---

14. There is some question about the authenticity of this passage because parallels in the other Gospels are lacking, but most scholars consider the saying genuine in the absence of textual evidence to the contrary. Whether authentic or not, its effect upon Christian thought warrants our dealing with it here.

true models for those who want to enter the Kingdom. Since Jesus appealed to God's primordial will for male and female as the foundation for marriage (i.e., that God intended man and woman to marry and become "one flesh" as part of his design for the world), and since he gave children a very high place in his thought, he could hardly have held at the same time that celibacy was the true way to "higher righteousness." His understanding of God's will would not have allowed such an inconsistency, and thus the traditional interpretation of this passage is untenable.

In light of this negative judgment, Matthew 19:10–12 is best interpreted in the same way as the passages just discussed, that is, as expressing Jesus' proclamation of the absolute supremacy of the claims of the Kingdom of God upon one's life. With respect to this passage, Jesus seems to be saying that if one cannot live up to God's original will for man (lifelong monogamy, as set forth in vv. 3–9), then it is better to remain unmarried (i.e., make oneself a "eunuch") than to disobey God's will by marrying and then divorcing. Given the views of his culture concerning the desirability of marriage, especially as the only means of gaining immortality (through one's children), remaining unmarried would indeed be a sacrifice on the same level as "losing one's life." But the reward is of course well worth it (19:29).

This interpretation suggests that Jesus, far from advocating celibacy, reaffirms the common opinion of his society: The first two categories of eunuchs certainly do not imply any positive valuation; and as for the third, just as he uses the renunciation of family relationships to illustrate what one might have to sacrifice if the Kingdom so demands, here he uses the example of a eunuch (as one of the worst possible states he and his hearers could think of) to indicate the extremes to which one might have to subject oneself in order to enter the Kingdom. Rather than disparaging sexuality and encouraging celibacy, then, this passage—seen in its own context and in that of Jesus' overall message— is neither a rejection of marriage nor a praise of the single state.

With a consideration of one final saying of Jesus that has also been used frequently to support the Church's anti-sexual stance, we shall conclude our look at these teachings of Jesus. In the most complete version, Luke 20:27–40, the Sadducees try to trap Jesus by asking about a woman who has had seven husbands: To whom will she belong in the resurrection? For our purposes the main point of

Jesus' response is, "The sons of this age marry and are given in marriage," but those who attain to the resurrection "neither marry nor are given in marriage, for they cannot die any more, because they are equal to angels and are sons of God" (vv. 34–36). Much has been written on this passage, and we cannot be concerned here with the details of interpretation.

Nevertheless, it is important to realize that in this passage Jesus' main point is to refute the Sadducees' denial of the resurrection (and of angels, according to Acts 23:8). To do this he simply turns the example they gave him against themselves. Furthermore, given the views of Jesus about marriage as a divine ordinance (for *this* life, at least), his basically positive attitude toward properly expressed sexuality, and the very high incidence of marriage in his culture, it does not seem reasonable to see in this passage a condemnation of marriage as inferior to celibacy because the "angels" do not marry. It may well be true that in the resurrection sexual differentiation will lose its great importance (though, since it is so central to one's personality, the "personal" nature of resurrection becomes questionable if sexuality is totally obliterated); if so, this is still no disparagement of sex and the sexual relationship as created by God *for this life*.

Also, Luke's inclusion of "for they cannot die any more," which follows the statement about not marrying, may imply simply that since immortality is a feature of the resurrection, marriage will no longer be needed in order to propagate the species. There may also be a suggestion that the exclusive nature of earthly relationships (of which marriage is surely the prime example) will be superseded by a larger community of affection. Finally, it is possible that Jesus is simply making the same point as in the immediately preceding pericope (the "render unto Caesar" story—Lk. 20:21–26): Do not try to apply to life in the Kingdom of God those categories which are applicable to this life.

The Sexuality of Jesus

Now that we have examined the specific statements of Jesus that contribute to our understanding of human sexuality, one further consideration must be mentioned, namely, the sexuality of Jesus himself. It is no exaggeration to say that this has probably been the most taboo topic in Christian thought for two thousand years, with devastating effects not only upon the Church's ability to think constructively about sexuality in general but also upon the credibility of its pronouncements to a secular world. In the traditional interpretation of the later Church, Jesus has been represented as an asthenic, non-emotional, "innocent" celibate who was far above anything so base as sexual feelings. With such a picture of the "model" for human life—the "most authentic man"—it is little wonder that the Church has been unable to reach any positive, affirmative view of human sexuality. Nor is it likely that Christian thinkers will be able to deal adequately *as Christians* with the pressing sexual issues faced by contemporary society as long as they continue to deny tacitly the sexual nature of the One they claim to follow. It is encouraging, therefore, that several steps have been taken to fill this major lacuna in Christian thought, and these efforts, whatever their shortcomings or extravagances, are to be commended for raising previously forbidden questions of great importance.[15]

Details of the problem of the sexuality of Jesus, especially regarding the ways in which he may have manifested it, are beyond the scope of this inquiry, which is primarily concerned with the New Testament record of Jesus' teachings on the subject in general. Although, as we have just seen, several statements attributed to Jesus in the Gospels broaden our understanding of human sexuality, in the New Testament there are simply no direct references to his sexuality or any expression of it. Thus all efforts to give a detailed description of Jesus' sexuality must remain speculative, and we cannot enter into this speculation. Since, however, it is impossible to separate the words totally from the one who utters them—especially in a religion so centered upon a person as is Christianity—several comments about the sexuality of Jesus are in order.

15. See, e.g., Tom F. Driver, "Sexuality and Jesus," in Martin E. Marty and Dean G. Peerman, eds., *New Theology No. 3* (New York: Macmillan Company, 1966); and two books by William E. Phipps, which have probably attracted the most attention: *Was Jesus Married?: The Distortion of Sexuality in the Christian Tradition* (New York: Harper & Row, 1970); and *The Sexuality of Jesus: Theological and Literary Perspectives* (New York: Harper & Row, 1973). An excellent treatment is given by Joseph Blenkinsopp in *Sexuality and the Christian Tradition*, Chapter 5, "The Silence of the Gospels." These works may be consulted for detailed and provocative presentations of a number of aspects of the question as well as for references to sources for further study. It is especially interesting that many of these references are to the realm of fiction, indicating that where theologians have feared to tread, novelists have been much less timid.

The first thing that must be said has already been mentioned and is self-evident, but it has been overlooked or intentionally ignored in much Christian writing on sex. Jesus was a Jew who, so to speak, lived in the Old Testament. That is, for him what we call the Old Testament was "the Bible," and the evidence is overwhelming that he found in the Jewish Scriptures *rightly interpreted* the basic norms of God's will for man. In addition to the numerous references to the Pentateuch and various prophets throughout his teachings, Jesus' acceptance and knowledge of the Torah are demonstrated in several other ways. In the only story we have of the "missing link" in Jesus' life, his childhood, Luke portrays him as listening to and questioning the biblical scholars in Jerusalem, who were "amazed at his understanding and his answers" (2:41–51).

Also, in his own ministry, he is addressed as "Rabbi," the title given to one learned in Jewish law; and there are a number of similarities between the picture of Jesus given in the Synoptic Gospels and that of other rabbis of his time in nonbiblical literature. Most important of all, however, are the explicit statements of Jesus himself asserting his adherence to the sacred writings of his fathers which we considered above; the most famous of these is undoubtedly Matthew 5:17: "Think not that I have come to abolish the law and the prophets; I have come not to abolish them but to fulfil them."

As a good Jew, then, well steeped in his heritage, Jesus would have held the overall world view—the attitude toward life and reality—of his tradition, the salient points of which have been presented in Chapters 1 and 2. Furthermore, as a Palestinian Jew, he would not have been likely to come under Hellenistic influence, with its dualistic outlook.[16] Jesus therefore surely affirmed the goodness of life and of all God's creation; this affirmation is explicitly attested to by his own enjoyment of life (see, e.g., Mt. 11:19) and by his references to natural events to make a point (e.g., Mt. 6:26, 28–30). More specifically, he also must have shared the Old Testament's healthy, affirmative view of sex and marriage, as we have seen illustrated by his teachings. Indeed, as a Jewish male, Jesus' whole background

16. By "dualism" I am referring to the separation of body and soul represented by Gnosticism and Manichaeanism which considers the body (and therefore sexuality) to be evil; I am not talking about the apocalyptic, cosmic dualism (e.g., light vs. darkness) which is evident in some later Jewish thought and in the Gospel of John.

taught him that sex within marriage was divinely created, ordained, and commanded, and therefore in a certain sense holy.

Given Jesus' affirmation of marriage and of the proper expression of sexuality which has been presented above, we can conclude that Jesus most likely held the view of sex prevalent in his tradition and that, unless he uttered a specific pronouncement on some issue, he probably accepted the Old Testament teaching as valid. This would almost certainly be the case for his general underlying beliefs. To assert the contrary is, in effect, to remove the basis for Christianity's acceptance of the Old Testament as Holy Scripture.

Another self-evident point—though more a theological necessity than an exegetical argument—needs to be stressed, again because it has been ignored almost totally in the Church's interpretations of Jesus. Stated plainly, if the cardinal doctrine of orthodox Christianity, the "fundamental Christian truth" in Brunner's words—the Incarnation—is to be valid, Jesus must have been a sexual being. If Jesus was "truly man" and "like us in all things, sin apart" (as the Chalcedonian Creed puts it), then clearly he possessed a sexual nature and experienced sexual feelings.[17] If this is denied, the doctrine of Christ's humanity becomes mere dogma—we do not know of "truly human" beings who are not sexual by nature, however they may choose to express or to refrain from expressing their sexuality.

Furthermore, Jesus' humanity is demonstrated in many ways in the Gospels, not least of which are the very human qualities he often displays: His anger is evident frequently, sometimes justified (Mk. 3:5; 11:15) and sometimes not (Mk. 11:12–14); he is depicted as tired, thirsty (Jn. 4:6–7), and hungry (Mt. 21:18); and he expresses pity, love, compassion, and sorrow (Mk. 1:41; Jn. 11:5, 33, 35). In the face of this evidence, it is unreasonable to deny *sexual* feelings to Jesus solely on *a priori* grounds based on one's own preconceived notions.

The traditional interpretation of Jesus, therefore, tends dangerously

---

17. The contention that Jesus' sinlessness meant that he was also sexless is not worthy of refutation since, as we have seen, his own tradition did not consider sex *per se* to be sinful; man may sin *with* sex, but it is *man* who sins, not Sex as some demonic power. Sex may indeed be a temptation, however, suggesting that Hebrews 4:15, which describes Jesus as "one who *in every respect* has been tempted as we are" (italics added), lends support to the point being made in the text.

toward Docetism, denying his full humanity in the one realm of sexuality. As Driver points out, this leads inexorably into Manichaean dualism: The only reason that can be given for the common view of Jesus as sexless is that he was above sexuality, but this denigrates sex to a position of inherent evil, a non-spiritual, worldly force that cannot be attributed to the loving Father's responsibility.[18] This heretical view is tacitly upheld by belief in Jesus' virgin birth, the evidence for which appears to be exceptionally slight. The assertion that God circumvented the normal, *sexual* method of procreation when he sent his Son into the world implicitly supports the view that such activity is evil and beneath the dignity of God. In fact, this doctrine, though long a part of orthodox faith, verges on the heretical itself in light of the prior importance of the Incarnation. To claim that God could not (or did not) become incarnate through the means he himself provided in creation is to call into serious question not only the sexuality of Jesus but, even more important, his very humanity.

Finally, concerning the question of how Jesus manifested his sexuality, the best conclusion we can reach is probably that it simply cannot be answered, however interesting the speculation is. There is perhaps some presumptive evidence that Jesus married at some time in his life,[19] but there is certainly nothing stated explicitly in the Gospels that provides a definitive answer to this question. Among the many possible reasons for this "silence of the Gospels," the one least subject to dispute seems to be that from the outset the synoptic tradition was ahistorical, if one means by "historical" a concern for the detailed "facts" of Jesus' life which fascinate biographers and readers today: The evangelists apparently were interested in the events that led to Jesus' death and resurrection, and these began only with his public ministry. Fortunately, in light of the points just presented, it is not necessary to decide this question in order to determine what is of importance to us. However Jesus chose to express his sexuality, as "perfect manhood" he shared in our sexual nature, and he most likely held basically the same healthy, positive attitude toward sex and marriage as did the tradition he inherited.

18. "Sexuality and Jesus," pp. 127–28.
19. William Phipps is of course the chief contemporary proponent of this view, especially in *Was Jesus Married?*

Summary

Jesus' teachings that pertain to human sexuality reveal a healthy, affirmative attitude on his part, as would be expected of someone from his background. He held marriage in high esteem as the divinely created pattern for the man-woman relationship, a union so intimate in fact that it cannot be broken by man. Furthermore, he affirmed the importance of women within God's creation, not just for their childbearing ability but as unique individuals worthy of respect and consideration in their own right. Although there are some statements in the Gospels that appear to disparage the family and sexual relationships, these are explained by Jesus' demands for the absolute supremacy of the Kingdom of God in one's life—a supremacy which indeed is the context for *all* his teachings. Finally, if one is to affirm the doctrine of the Incarnation, it must be clearly stated that Jesus himself was a sexual being, although from the available evidence we are unaware of the ways in which he may have manifested his sexuality. Admittedly, our records of Jesus do not provide a great deal of information about sexuality, but what they do offer is overwhelmingly positive, and there is certainly no hint at all of any disparagement of this crucial aspect of man's being.

4

New Testament Development:
Paul

The apostle Paul, the other major New Testament figure, appears to hold a considerably different attitude toward sexuality from that of Jesus. So prevalent has this opinion been in the traditional interpretations of his writings that today Paul's attitude is commonly held to be the major cause of the distortion of Jesus' positive attitude toward sexuality. Moreover, Paul is considered by many to be the primary source of certain beliefs and practices of the Christian Church that have caused untold suffering. Among these are the Church's basically anti-sexual stance, which implies that celibacy is the "true Christian way"; an obsession with sexual sins, often to the neglect of other more subtle "sins of the spirit"; and the sanction and practice of male dominance and female subservience.

These are serious charges against the man whom many consider to be more important in the formulation, and certainly in the spread, of the Christian faith than Jesus himself. Clearly we must come to grips with Paul's thought if we want to reach a viable understanding of sexuality that finds its foundation in the historical documents of Christianity. Without dwelling on the various misinterpretations of Paul reflected in the views just cited, let us examine his statements that are pertinent to human sexuality.[1]

---

1. Unfortunately, we will be hampered in this effort by at least two major obstacles, which should constantly be borne in mind: First, as suggested earlier, so much has been said and written about Paul's views, and certain interpretations have become so ingrained in our traditions, that it is very difficult to cut through this accretion to what is of value in his own words; and second, Paul's attitude and expression are peculiarly complex and at times apparently contradictory (or at best paradoxical), a fact noted in his own time—cf. 2 Peter 3:15b–16: "Our beloved brother Paul wrote to you . . . , speaking of this as he does in all his letters. There are *some things in them hard to understand*, which the ignorant and unstable twist to their own destruction, as they do the other scriptures" (italics added).

Paul's Background

In the first place, it must be pointed out that much of what was said concerning Jesus' background and presuppositions is equally applicable to Paul. By his own affirmation, Paul was a strict Jew before his conversion, in fact a Pharisee and a son of Pharisees (Acts 23:6; cf. 26:4–11), and in Galatians 1:14 he says, "I advanced in Judaism beyond many of my own age among my people, so extremely zealous was I for the traditions of my fathers" (cf. v. 13 and Phil. 3:4–6). Despite his conversion, there is no indication that the deeply ingrained views of his heritage were lost, and he clearly relied heavily on the Hebrew Scriptures for his understanding of God's will for man.[2]

We would therefore expect certain attitudes on Paul's part with respect to several issues of importance to us: Sexuality would be seen as God-given and thus good *when used in accord with* God's will; marriage would be held to be the pattern God intended for the man-woman relationship, an unbreakable union of two into "one flesh"; and women would be valued for their maternal, domestic, and related functions but still considered inherently subordinate to men. In general, as we shall see, on none of these issues did Paul deviate substantially from the traditions which he spent a large part of his life learning, living, and protecting.

On the other hand, Paul, unlike Jesus, did not spend his entire life in Palestine, exclusively among Jews only.[3] Paul was more "cosmopolitan," a world traveler who spoke and wrote Greek, and who there-

---

2. Victor Paul Furnish presents a concise and balanced summary of Paul's indebtedness to his Judaic background in *Theology and Ethics in Paul* (Nashville: Abingdon Press, 1968), pp. 28–44; hereafter cited as *Paul*.

3. This difference in the *curricula vitae* of the two may go a long way toward explaining the great discrepancy between Jesus' few, practically incidental references to sexual matters and Paul's numerous, forceful statements. Jesus clearly saw his mission as exclusively to Israel (cf. Mt. 15:24), which had very high sexual standards for the time relative to the surrounding Gentile world. Jesus therefore could concentrate on the sins of religious pride, hypocrisy, and arrogance which he saw all around him. In contrast, Paul was called as the "Apostle to the Gentiles" (cf. Rom. 1:14), people whose sexual mores were generally lower than those of the Jews, and thus many of his converts had trouble understanding, much more fulfilling, the rigid moral demands of their new faith. The influence of dualistic anthropologies tended to make the Gentiles see sexuality in ways totally alien to Paul's outlook as a Jew. Furthermore, given several distinctively Christian elements in Paul's understanding of sex to be discussed shortly, it is not surprising that he felt the need to deal often and strongly with sexual improprieties and misunderstandings in his congregations.

fore must have appropriated not only Hellenistic terminology and style but concepts as well. Furthermore, it is important to note that the Jewish Scriptures which Paul relied upon so heavily were themselves in Greek, with the necessarily consequent influence of Greek thought forms and language. Finally, as Furnish notes, the Judaism that Paul had learned was neither pure Old Testament nor Palestinian Judaism but Diaspora Judaism, which was heavily influenced by Hellenistic thought and language. The conclusion to be drawn, then, seems to be simply that Paul's thought and mode of expression stemmed from a pluralistic and complex background.[4]

Nevertheless, it is essential to an understanding of Paul (and of the misinterpretations of him) to realize that when he did appropriate words or concepts from Hellenism, his Jewish background surely led him frequently to interpret them differently from their use by native Greeks—he must have understood them from his Hebraic point of view. Although Paul may have used some of the same language as Hellenistic philosophy, this does not mean at all that the *content* given to this form by the two was identical. Paul appears to have imparted to most of these shared words and concepts a considerably different meaning, often to the confusion of those to whom he wrote, who had learned the words with other associations and connotations. Unfortunately, most of the early interpreters of Christianity also were from purely Hellenistic backgrounds and did not share Paul's underlying Hebraic presuppositions.

It is therefore not surprising that many of the words and ideas appropriated from Hellenism by Paul, when interpreted by Greek minds steeped in dualistic world views, took on overtones unintended by Paul, leading to the serious distortion of his thought evident today. As Brevard Childs concludes, when Paul's statements were separated from their Old Testament roots in the spread of Christianity through the Greaco-Roman world, an attitude toward sexuality and marriage developed that was not at all in keeping with the Judaic assumptions from which Paul operated.[5] Thus it is especially crucial for us to keep firmly in mind Paul's Old Testament background as a balance to the traditional interpretations of his position through Hellenistically

4. *Paul*, pp. 44, 65; Furnish's summary of the Hellenistic influence upon Paul is on pp. 44–50.
5. *Biblical Theology in Crisis* (Philadelphia: Westminster Press, 1970), p. 199.

influenced presuppositions. Only in this way can we be fair to Paul himself and gain the truly valuable insights he offers us.[6]

It is also important in understanding Paul's statements which are pertinent to sexuality to be aware of the nature of the medium through which he expressed his thoughts. Unlike most current theological-ethical writing, the only extant records we have of Paul's ideas are occasional letters (it is generally agreed that the speeches by Paul in Acts are creations by Luke, not verbatim records of Paul's own words), written hastily to particular congregations, usually with particular concerns in mind. This is especially so of Paul's most extended treatment of sexual matters, Chapters 5–7 of 1 Corinthians.[7] He was not concerned to set forth polished theological reflection, critically and deliberately honed to preciseness of expression; rather he wanted to instruct his various churches on the topics most important to them at the time, and his sense of pastoral urgency is often evident. Thus it is unfair to Paul and untrue to legitimate biblical interpretation to try to find in his letters a systematic legal code to govern Christian behavior in every situation.

One general aspect of Paul's theology bears heavily upon our final interpretation of his position. Whatever the outcome of the scholarly debate about Paul's belief in the Hellenistic concept of a "natural law" according to which every human being can intuitively know right or wrong, it is clear from Paul's writing that he thinks he knows what God's will is and that this will can be discerned by observing "nature."[8]

6. Childs uses this very issue to make the methodological point of the necessity for the theologian to read the New Testament in light of the Old, thereby avoiding two faulty hermeneutical moves—either absolutizing Paul's ethic for Christians in every age, or dismissing it as merely the view of a time- and place-bound individual which is therefore useless in a different time and place. If one affirms the canonical authority of Paul's writings but examines them in the perspective and balance of other witnesses, a third alternative becomes available for the interpretation of Scripture. *Ibid.*, pp. 199–200. This book is an attempt to carry out Childs' suggestion.

7. Indeed, Chapter 6 contains an excellent illustration of the hasty, unpolished nature of Paul's letters: Into a relatively connected consideration of sexual morality, Paul inserts an extraneous discussion about the settling of lawsuits between Christians (vv. 1–8). Apparently the mention of judgment (5:12–13) reminded him of this particular problem, and he dealt with it while it was on his mind.

8. This is the case in principle, at least. But because man is now under sin, his perception is blurred, and even if he discerns aright what God's will for him is, he cannot bring his *own* will to do what he knows is right. Cf. Rom. 7:19: "For I do not do the good I want, but the evil I do not want is what I do."

In Romans 1:18–23, Paul condemns the suppression of truth by men who know what God expects of them:

> For what can be known about God is plain to them, because God has shown it to them. Ever since the creation of the world his invisible nature, namely, his eternal power and deity, has been clearly perceived in the things that have been made. So they are without excuse (vv. 19–20).

Paul therefore clearly implies that men can "know God" and his will for them by examining the "things that have been made," and this seems especially to be the case with respect to sexuality: Verses 26–27, describing the exchange of sexual relations "in accordance with nature" for those "contrary to nature," can be seen as a specific illustration of the general point made in verse 20.

Furthermore, Paul is not averse to commending whatever is generally recognized as natural, human excellence (Phil. 4:8), nor does he hesitate to conclude a theological argument with a final appeal to what is "proper" and natural (1 Cor. 11:13–14). Although he may have been mistaken as to what is really "natural" because of the limited biological and anthropological knowledge of his day, the point remains that Paul thought he could discover God's will in the order of creation, probably because the "new creation" in Christ is once again in harmony with God's original intention. We thus see in this a point of affinity with Jesus, whose recognition of the connection between the moral order and the natural order has already been discussed.

Paul believed that in Christ the primordial will of God concerning men's relationships with one another and with nature had been restored, and on this basis he took a stance of great significance for an interpretation of his statements about sexuality. Scattered throughout Paul's writings (and those attributed to him)[9] are assertions that God's creation, the material world, is unquestionably good and is to be

9. It is necessary to comment here on the question of Pauline authorship of the various New Testament epistles. It is outside the scope of this book to deal definitively with such technical matters, and it is not possible to look at each letter individually. Although the arguments on each side of the question concerning any specific letter are often strong, my research has led to the conclusions which Werner Georg Kümmel draws in *Introduction to the New Testament,* founded by Paul Feine and Johannes Behm, completely reedited by Kümmel, A. J. Mattill, Jr., trans. (14th rev. ed.; Nashville: Abingdon Press, 1966): Galatians, Romans, 1 and 2 Corinthians, 1 and 2 Thessalonians, Phillipians, Colossians, and Philemon are Pauline in origin, whereas Hebrews, Ephesians, and the Pastorals are not.

accepted with gratitude and enjoyed through proper use. In this view, Paul stands in the best tradition of Old Testament Judaism and of Jesus, as we have seen. In Romans 14:14a, Paul states unequivocally that he knows and is persuaded in the Lord Jesus Christ "that nothing is unclean in itself," a view developed in 1 Corinthians 10:25–31: Since "the earth is the Lord's, and everything in it," the believer can "partake with thankfulness" without fear of being denounced because of that for which he gives thanks.

In Colossians 2:20–23, Paul refutes the ascetic "heretics" at Colossae and gives Christians leave to use what God has created for them: Through Christ one is freed from legal restrictions upon the use of material things because they play no role in salvation (although, of course, one is expected to make the right use of them *because* of one's belief in Christ). In short, as the author of 1 Timothy puts it, "everything created by God is good, and nothing is to be rejected if it is received with thanksgiving" (4:4). Sex and marriage are expressly included in this "everything" since the forbidding of marriage is one of the two specific acts for which the "liars" are condemned (v. 3). Obviously, this does not mean that *any* action is permitted, but 1 Timothy does reflect Paul's own belief that the appropriate use and enjoyment of God's material creation is to be encouraged. Thus there is good reason to claim, even before considering any of Paul's statements specifically dealing with sexuality, that he could not have been the doctrinaire "anti-sexualist" of popular opinion.

Paul's View of Sexuality and Marriage

There are two areas of Paul's thought that are especially pertinent to our effort to determine the New Testament's understanding of human sexuality: his view of sex and marriage and his attitude toward women. Although the two cannot be separated (as, indeed, they cannot be isolated from his overall theological stance), for clarity of explication it is helpful to examine each in turn. Paul's single extended discussion of sexual matters, 1 Corinthians 5–7, will serve as a useful format for examining his specific statements about sexuality and marriage.

1 Corinthians 5

In Chapter 5, Paul addresses himself to a specific case of immorality, as he does elsewhere in a more general way (cf., e.g., Rom. 1:24–32;

2 Cor. 12:20–21; Gal. 5:19–21; and 1 Thess. 4:1–8). It is important to note first that Paul makes clear that he does not expect his readers to withdraw from the "immoral of this world" (v. 10), thereby obviating any claim that he advocated other-worldly asceticism. More significant is the clarification he offers of what he does mean: By his analogy to leaven, he points out that one such case of immorality, openly committed and even bragged about, can insidiously permeate and destroy the church. This must not be permitted.

Thus in this chapter Paul does not suggest retreat from the world but expressly forbids it, and he condemns only immorality (not sexuality properly expressed) because of its detrimental effect upon the community. Indeed, this is the crucial issue: As with the Old Testament and Jesus, Paul's concern is with the *misuse* of sexuality, not sexuality *per se*. Since "nothing is unclean in itself," it is only its improper use that makes it so, and this is especially the case with sex.

Even in Paul's lists of vices cited above, sexual sins are only a few among many, and it is always the *improper* use of sex that is condemned—he clearly was not preoccupied with sex as the "root of all sins." Furthermore, as 5:6–7, 11 make clear, Paul did not share the prevalent Hellenistic view that sexual sins were private, personal vices which the *individual* had to avoid or overcome for his or her own salvation. Apparently for Paul, the evil of sexual sins was their effect *upon others,* in this case specifically the community of believers who together comprise the body of Christ. Given Paul's distinctive "corporate theology," this emphasis is not surprising.

1 Corinthians 6

The concerns and themes of Chapter 5 are continued in Chapter 6, and are augmented by some crucial new ones. Although often seen as indicating a negative attitude toward sex, this chapter clearly shows that, again, Paul's interest lay with urging the *right use* of a God-given gift. Passing over verses 1–8 (which we have seen to be an extraneous insertion that illustrates the hasty way in which Paul's letters were written), we find Paul once more cataloguing vices that prevent entrance into the Kingdom of God. Here also he merely lists several of a sexual nature along with other more general ones (vv. 9–10). In verse 11, Paul suggests what many scholars consider to be the major motivation for moral conduct for the apostle, which he amplifies in verses 12–20 (esp. 19b–20): God's freely given saving gift in Christ imposes upon the believer the obligation to fulfill what he owes to God, and here we see that Paul continues the emphasis of Jesus upon the inseparability of religion and morality. This obligation, of course, manifests itself in the realm of sexual morality as elsewhere, and Paul devotes the rest of Chapter 6 to an important explication of this principle.

Apparently there was a faction within the church at Corinth which retained the Greek dualistic anthropology that radically separated body and soul. This group argued, therefore, that what the body does has no effect on the spirit as long as one professes belief in Christ and otherwise cares for the soul. This, of course, meant that these people in the Corinthian church believed themselves to be free to indulge in whatever sexual practices they wished. Indeed, the motto of these "Christian libertines" was "All things are lawful for me" (v. 12). They supported this position with the naturalistic assertion, "Food is meant for the stomach and the stomach for food" (v. 13); this is an obvious claim that satisfying sexual desires has no more moral significance than eating when one feels hungry since the body, like food, perishes while the soul lives on.

To the first claim, Paul responded with a capsule summary of his concept of true freedom in Christ: Granted, all things may be lawful "but not all things are helpful"—one must not become enslaved by anything. Here again the emphasis is on the *right use* of sexuality, its use for the purposes and in the ways which God intended without letting it become a preoccupation and ruling force in one's life. As for the claim that sex is as natural as eating, Paul answered with a classic statement of the sanctity of the body, a statement which contains several elements worthy of closer examination.

— In the first place, Paul argued from both his Judaic background and his Christian faith and forcefully reaffirmed a major Hebraic contribution to anthropology and psychology, namely, the rejection of the dualistic partition of man into body and soul. Paul, who has been maligned as an ascetic sex hater, is chiefly responsible for strengthening and giving wider circulation to this idea that is central to a Christian understanding of sexuality. For Paul, it is simply not true that what a person *does* has no effect upon who that person *is*, because, in fact, one *is* what one *does*. This inseparability is evident throughout Paul's writings in his stress upon the necessity for faith to become active in love (cf. Gal. 5:6).

Sexual expression, therefore, involves the *whole* person, soul included, and not just the sex organs. Since the dichotomy between body and soul is invalid in Paul's opinion, there is no question that one's outer behavior can enslave the "inner self" because the two are really the same; one's behavior therefore *must* have an effect on the "self." In the context of 1 Corinthians 6:12–20, Furnish's observation is apposite: As Paul made clear in Chapter 5, the Christian is still very much in the world and thus subject in earthly relationships to God's sovereignty—since, as we just saw, one's body is the outward manifestation of one's entire being, the use one makes of it manifests one's response to God's claim,[10] which is Paul's continuing theme.

Since, therefore, body and spirit are inseparable, "the body [like the soul] is not meant for immorality, but for the Lord, and the Lord for the body." The ultimate proof of this sanctity of the body is that "God raised the Lord and will also raise us up by his power" (vv. 13b–14). If one joins himself with a prostitute, he becomes one body with her, but one united with Christ is one spirit with him (vv. 16–17). For Paul, with his high view of the sanctity of marriage and the "one-flesh" union, joining oneself with a prostitute is therefore intolerable.

In verse 20b, Paul concludes the chapter with a final example of the seriousness with which he held this view: "So glorify God in your body" (cf. Rom. 12:1 and Phil. 1:20). He certainly did not mean by this any form of cultic sexual activity, and thus the apparent meaning is simply that the body is the only means we have through which to manifest our praise of God—glorifying God is not a strictly "spiritual" activity but a "somatic" one, and the believer will use his body accordingly. In short, Paul is saying that even more important than words in the praise of God, one's actions—the use one makes of one's body—are what really matter, a position with which Jesus certainly would have agreed. Thus this stress on the psychophysical unity of man precludes attaching an inferior valuation to the body and allows a greatly heightened view of human sexuality.

A closely related concept is Paul's assertion that the body is a "temple of the Holy Spirit within you" (v. 19; cf. 3:16–17), clearly a very high and hardly ascetic view of the body. The rich "body imagery" employed by Paul with respect to Christ and the Church cannot be examined in detail here (cf. Rom. 12:4–5; 1 Cor. 12:12–27;

10. *Paul*, p. 170.

Col. 1:18; 3:5; and its deutero-Pauline use in Eph. 4:15–16 and 5:23–32); but his use of the words *flesh, spirit,* and *body* requires some consideration. Although Paul's anthropology is a difficult region of his thought, there is considerable scholarly agreement about what he meant by these often misinterpreted terms. As pointed out earlier, when viewed through Hellenistic presuppositions, Paul frequently appears to disparage sex and to encourage asceticism, and this is especially so in this case: By contrasting life "in the flesh" with life "in the Spirit," he seems to follow the dualistic view that the body, and specifically sexual desires, are the center of all evil. An examination of two passages in Galatians quickly shows the fallacy in this interpretation.

In Galatians 5:16–24, where the contrast between life "in the flesh" and "in the Spirit" is clearly drawn, Paul proscribes fifteen "works of the flesh," of which only three (*porneia, akartharsia, aselgeia*) have any sexual reference at all and only two others (*methai, kōmoi*) relate particularly to what we would call "physical" desires. Indeed, fully two-thirds of these "fleshly" sins are those which come "out of the heart of man," as Jesus put it in Mark 7:21; but these are hardly sensual passions in the normal sense. Furthermore, in Galatians 3, Paul eloquently presents his case against salvation by the law, which was being advocated even for Christians by certain "Judaizing" teachers in Galatia. Paul asked his converts pointedly in verse 3, "Are you so foolish? Having begun with the Spirit, are you now ending with the flesh?" He obviously meant by "beginning with the Spirit" their conversion through "hearing with faith"; in the context "the flesh" refers to adherence to the Mosaic law, which would hardly have led to *sensual* excesses. When one recalls also that Paul used "in the flesh" in a neutral sense merely to mean "earthly existence,"[11] it is clear that he never intended to advocate a dualistic scheme in which "the flesh" is considered inherently evil. What, then, did he mean?

The concept of psychophysical unity provides the answer to this question. The person is seen as a unified being; and body, flesh, and spirit are not separate elements which comprise the individual but rather the *total* individual considered from various angles with different emphases. The "flesh" is not one part of man (e.g., his "physical" side

11. Cf. 2 Cor. 10:3 and especially Gal. 2:20, where Paul says "the life I now live *in the flesh* I live *by faith*" (italics added).

opposed to his "intellectual," as in body/mind dualisms) but rather a description of a "mode of existence." The "flesh" signifies man in his mortal nature as a creature, finite and limited, frail and fundamentally dependent; thus Paul could use it neutrally. The flesh becomes sinful, as reflected in Paul's negative references, only when man sets it up as his "ultimate concern" and regulates his life according to its values and desires, letting it dominate him. One tries to live self-sufficiently, on his own resources, declaring his independence of God and setting himself up as the standard against which to judge past acts and from which to gain future hope.[12]

The "body" is merely man's actual, historical manifestation, in effect the entire self, and as such, of course, it is the means by which the "flesh" expresses its dominion. Life "in the Spirit," on the other hand, means that one's life is regulated by faith in God's act through Christ rather than by one's own standards and desires. There is perhaps a duality in Paul's thought, but it is the Hebraic one of good and evil contending within an individual, "two impulses" at war within one's heart. These forces are not divided, as in Hellenistic dualism, between two parts of an individual, such as body and soul, but rather struggle for control of the *whole* person; and it is clear that for Paul victory of "the flesh" meant something quite different from failure to overcome one's sexual desires.

A further element in 1 Corinthians 6 that expresses Paul's belief in the sanctity of the body is his quotation of the same Genesis passage (2:24) which Jesus used in his affirmation of God's original intention for marriage. Significantly, though, Paul extended the "one-flesh" concept to casual coitus with a prostitute, with whom "one becomes one body" (v. 16). This seems to move a step beyond Old Testament usage, which regarded the one-flesh union to be the result of the total commitment of husband and wife, and Jesus certainly understood the passage to apply to marriage.

Nevertheless, given the profound understanding Paul had of the importance of sex, it is not unreasonable to suppose that he meant what he wrote; and his claim that *even* a transitory, commercial sexual encounter inextricably binds two people represents a considerable heightening of the importance of the sexual act. Such an

12. Furnish, *Paul*, p. 137. The significance of Paul's statement in Gal. 3:3 is apparent here, equating as it does living "in the flesh" with zeal for the law.

emphasis would be well within the parenetic purpose of this chapter, especially since some of those to whom it was addressed saw nothing at all wrong with sexual indulgence. For Paul, since the body is intended to be used to glorify God as a "temple of the Holy Spirit," it was unthinkable to consider uniting it with a prostitute.[13]

It is abundantly clear, then, that 1 Corinthians 6, far from disparaging sex, presents Paul's exceptionally high view of it—a view which was based primarily on his understanding that sex was created by God to serve a unitive function for man and woman, uniting them in their *total* beings and fulfilling both. Paul was extremely sensitive to offenses against this relational function and used as his fundamental sanction God's redemption and ultimate resurrection of the body through the saving work of Christ. Sexuality is one of God's most powerful and therefore most important gifts to humanity, and it is the *misuse* of this capacity, not sex itself as created by God, that offended Paul and called down his judgment. Sexuality must be used rightly: It is to this question that Paul turned in Chapter 7, in which he addressed a group of Christians who apparently had ascetic leanings.

1 Corinthians 7

1 Corinthians 7 is the section of Paul's writings most often cited as indicative of his negative view of sex and marriage. The chapter is filled with problems, both technical and interpretive; yet it contains profound insights and intimations about sexuality and the marriage relationship. As interesting as many of these aspects are, however, we

---

13. Our understanding of the important concept of "one flesh" is aided by a brief consideration of another idea of Paul that is similar and even explicitly related by him in 1 Cor. 6:16–17: The concept of the believer's *union with Christ* in his death and resurrection. In 1 Cor. 6:17, Paul uses the fact that "he who is united to the Lord becomes one spirit with him" as the reason not to become one body with a prostitute through coitus. This juxtaposition indicates that Paul saw some affinity between the two "unions." Furnish states that it is a misinterpretation of the union with Christ to see it as a "mystical union": The believer's identity is not lost and "his being is not merged with Christ's but rather belongs to Christ." The union is always described in "*relational,* not *mystical* categories," nor, we might add, *ontological* ones. *Paul,* p. 176. By analogy, then, the "one-flesh" union is not a mystical union, an ontological bond or real merging of two individuals but rather a *relationship,* with the two partners *belonging* to each other in a profound, unique way that cannot come about through any other means. With this understanding, the question of divorce can be dealt with: It is still against God's will as the dissolution of a unique relationship but it is no longer a problem of sundering, or trying to sunder, a real ontological merger of two separate identities.

can consider only the salient ones here. At the outset it may be useful to reiterate a point made earlier: It is especially important to keep in mind that Paul is responding to specific questions asked of him (v. 1a) in a particular place and time and that he is not primarily concerned to set forth general and permanently binding rules.

Indeed, this circumstance suggests an interpretation of Chapter 7 which is totally at odds with the traditional one. This reinterpretation sees verse 1b (which lacks the copula in the Greek) as Paul's *restatement* of one of the matters about which the Corinthians wrote. It is then translated either as a question or, by supplying the infinitive of "to be," as an indirect statement dependent upon "wrote" (i.e., "Now concerning the matters about which you wrote, [first,] that it is well for a man not to touch a woman.").[14] The immediate advantage of this interpretation is that it allows the imperatives of the next two verses (translated "should" in the RSV) to be understood as imperatives without contradicting what Paul has just said. Furthermore, it brings Paul's position here into harmony with his basically positive view of sexuality.

It is, of course, impossible to deny that Paul expressed a preference for the single state in this chapter—whether it is a preference for "celibacy" *per se*, as usually interpreted, is another question however. That is, Paul does not seem to be recommending that the single person remain so because of any inherent evil in sexuality or inferiority in marriage (cf., e.g., 1 Thess. 4:3–4, where "taking a wife" is equated in some sense with the "will of God"). Indeed, he expressly *forbids* the married to become single. The apparent reason for this is that, as almost all scholars agree, Paul's thought was largely determined by his very strong eschatological expectation of the imminent return of Christ (cf. vv. 26, 29a, 31b). This perspective, difficult to comprehend today, meant that *all* features of normal life become secondary in expectation of the *eschaton*. Paul's recommendation not to marry, then, seems to have two eschatologically motivated thrusts: first, that Christians should be totally free to serve the Lord as Paul himself was (vv. 32b, 34b); and second, that unmarried persons would be spared anxieties about spouses in the end-time (vv. 28b, 33, 34c).

14. For a convincing presentation of this interpretation, see William F. Orr, "Paul's Treatment of Marriage in 1 Corinthians 7," *Pittsburgh Perspective*, VII (September, 1967), 5–22; hereafter cited as "Paul."

Paul's preference for the single state was clearly prompted by this strong sense of urgency; and it seems certain that if he had really held the negative view of sex which is usually attributed to him on the basis of this chapter—if he had not had his Judaically inspired healthy valuation of sex—he would simply have urged Christians to renounce sex altogether. Paul, however, held too high a view of sex as part of God's good creation to do this, and even though "the form of this world is passing away," he insisted that both men and women had the right to marry if they so chose (v. 28a).[15]

What then did Paul say about sexuality and marriage that can contribute positively to our understanding of human sexuality? Of great importance is his stress on the relational, unitive aspect of sex over the procreative, a significant shift from the Old Testament emphasis along the lines which we have already seen in Jesus' statements. In fact, Paul does not mention procreation at all in any of his discussions of sexuality. His extension of the "one-flesh" idea (1 Cor. 6:15–17) and his belief in the permanence and indissolubility of marriage (Rom. 7:2–3; 1 Cor. 7:10–13, 39) indicate this side of his thought; the clearest illustration of his recognition of the nonprocreative importance of sex, however, appears in 1 Cor. 7:3–4.

Here, instead of commending ascetic practices in marriage (as one who grudgingly allowed sex only for its necessary procreative function would be expected to do), Paul clearly forbade them, except for brief periods when *both* partners agree to abstain for devotional purposes. He thus extended his understanding of the one flesh of marriage into a statement of the absolute equality and mutuality of the partners in conjugal relations. It is not unreasonable to imagine that Paul might have thought, "Since a couple becomes truly 'one flesh' in coitus, clearly neither partner alone can control the unity that ensues since it consists of both of them—the husband has a right to the body of his

15. Orr offers the practical observation that since Paul was mistaken (i.e., the end did not come in his time and has not yet come), a "little revision" may be needed in the principles Paul enunciated based on his expectations. See "Paul," p. 19. It is also worthy of note that in each instance in Chapter 7 in which Paul advocated not marrying, he was careful to state that this was a *personal opinion*, not a command from the Lord: "I say, not the Lord . . . ." Furthermore, in v. 35, he made even clearer that he was only *recommending* based on his understanding of the times, not *commanding* based on apostolic authority: "I say this for your own benefit, *not to lay any restraint* upon you . . ." (italics added). The one "command of the Lord" he cited (vv. 10–11) gives implicit honor to the marriage relationship by recalling (probably) Jesus' prohibition of divorce in Mk. 10:2–9.

wife and the wife to that of her husband." To surrender authority over one's body suggests that the spouse has an equal right to emotional and sexual fulfillment in the marital relationship, and this right is obligatory *upon both* at all times, with the one exception noted. This principle is somewhat surprising given general first-century attitudes, and it is certainly alien to the popular picture of Paul.

We should not assume from this, however, that for Paul marriage was merely a physical, genital relationship designed only to satisfy passions (despite 1 Cor. 7:2, 5, and especially 9); nor that it was just a necessary evil (despite vv. 8–9, 26, and 40). That it was considerably more is shown by the extraordinary principle set forth in verse 14, of which traditional Christian thought on marriage seems to have taken little notice: "For the unbelieving husband is consecrated through his wife, and the unbelieving wife is consecrated through her husband" (here again, incidentally, we see Paul's emphasis on mutuality). Whatever Paul meant exactly by the word *consecrated* in this context,[16] elsewhere it means for him a special relationship to God and not any particular moral quality achieved by the individual: Consecration consists of being "set apart" for God's service, being "made holy" to him.[17] This sanctification normally requires the obedient response in faith of the believer. But in marriage, according to Paul, the union between husband and wife is so intimate, the "one flesh" so complete, that the nonbeliever is somehow sanctified through the faith of the believer.

This in itself is a radical concept, but what is even more significant for our inquiry is that Paul thus expressly included the *bodies* of Christians in the process of religious sanctification; therefore marriage and sexuality cannot be merely profane, necessities of a "fallen" world, but share in the "new creation." This sanctification must be sexual in some sense because, as we have seen, for Paul the "one flesh" comes about through coitus and nothing else. Paul made clear

16. According to Walter Bauer, the word means to "include in the inner circle of what is holy, in both relig. [sic] and moral uses of the word." See *A Greek-English Lexicon of the New Testament and Other Early Christian Literature*, William F. Arndt and F. Wilbur Gingrich, trans. (Chicago: University of Chicago Press, 1957), p. 8. Paul uses the same word to refer to those "sanctified in Christ Jesus" (1 Cor. 1:2), "in the name of the Lord Jesus Christ and in the Spirit of our God" (6:11), and by "the God of peace" (1 Thess. 5:23).

17. Furnish, *Paul*, p. 155. Furnish calls the distinction between justification and sanctification which is sometimes detected in Paul's thought "specious." See p. 154.

in verses 3–5 that marriage necessarily includes coitus, and thus he cannot mean that the consecration of the nonbelieving spouse (which occurs in marriage) takes place simply by "osmosis" through physical proximity, and even less by active proselytizing on the believer's part. For Paul, the union of two in one flesh—the highest expression of human sexuality when it occurs within the context of the deep and total relationship that is marriage—is of such a nature that a believer can bring about the religious sanctification of a nonbelieving spouse. In a sense, then, Paul considers coitus (and therefore human sexuality in general) to be "sacramental," to be a channel through which the material is used to bring about spiritual results—in this case, the sanctification of the marriage partner.

Paul's basically positive view of the marriage relationship is echoed elsewhere in the New Testament, especially in 1 Timothy and Ephesians (both of which reflect Pauline thought). In 1 Timothy 3, bishops and deacons are commanded to be "husbands of one wife" (vv. 2, 12), and the practical value of marriage is stressed by suggesting that those who care for God's church must be able to show their ability by managing their own households well (vv. 4–5, 12). Ephesians 5:21–33 contains an especially ennobling statement of Christian marriage and uses marriage as a symbol of the relationship between Christ and his Church. This passage in Ephesians also continues the concern of 1 Corinthians 7:3–4 by stressing the mutuality of marriage (cf. v. 21: "Be subject to one another . . .") and the extremely close relationship between husband and wife which is brought about by coitus (vv. 28–31).

To recapitulate briefly, we have seen that the attitudes of both the Old Testament and Jesus are decidedly positive toward human sexuality and express concern only that this God-given gift be used *properly*. Neither suggests at all that sexuality should not be used because of some inherent evil attributed to it. As for Paul, it has been shown that his view of sex is also basically positive, even when he recommends not marrying in 1 Corinthians 7. He certainly indicated his awareness of possible abuses and temptations of sex, but this was no more than a legitimate recognition of its power and importance, and not any disparagement of sexuality *per se*. There may indeed have been an ascetic bent in Paul personally which was absent in his tradition, Jewish or Christian. When he wrote as a theologian and ethicist, therefore, Paul transcended his own personal proclivity for the sake of the theological truth he wrote to maintain, as illustrated, for example, by his broadening of the "one-flesh" idea, his view of the body as a temple for the Holy Spirit, and his doctrine of "conjugal sanctification."

Paul's Attitude Toward Women

With respect to another aspect of his thought—his attitude toward women—Paul adopted the basic view of his Judaic tradition but failed to evidence the same freedom from it, in this instance, as did Jesus. The condemnation of the Apostle for his antisexualism, in fact, is rivaled only by the vilification heaped upon him for his antifeminism. The actual situation, however, appears to be that Paul's attitude was quite mixed. Perhaps on this issue, more than any other, it is impossible to say what "Paul's position" is; and here, more clearly than anywhere else, certain elements of his Christian faith collide most violently and perplexingly with his deeply ingrained Judaic upbringing.

A careful perusal of Paul's epistles leaves no doubt that he felt very great affection and appreciation for the women of his churches. They were more active than would be expected given the Jewish and Greek customs of the day; and in the "personal" sections of all Paul's letters, women are among those greeted or referred to warmly, often in higher proportions than one would suppose likely within the prevailing social patterns (cf. Rom. 16).

Without trying to make too much of these references, one can at least assert that no confirmed misogynist would have been likely to have so many female friends and coworkers, or to have spoken so highly of them. Paul's was definitely not a grudging acceptance of inferior beings. Moreover, there is no indication that these women were merely members with no responsibilities: In verse 1, Phoebe is said to be a "deaconess," and she must have been a highly valued and trusted partner in his ministry since Paul urges the Romans to "receive her in the Lord . . . for she has been a helper of many and of myself as well." In verse 6, another woman, Mary, is commended for having "worked hard among you."

On the other hand, it is undeniable that Paul also clearly stated the view that women should be subordinate, especially in 1 Corinthians 11:3–16, 14:33b–35, and Colossians 3:18–19. Georgia Harkness rightly laments that these are the passages that are so familiar and so often quoted rather than those in which Paul expresses his appreciation of women; and even today, when a secular world rejects the Bible as a guide and smiles patronizingly at Paul's naivete, the effects of his negative statements about women linger indirectly in practically all male-female relationships.[18]

It is apparent, then, that theological ethics must come to grips with these statements that disparage half of the sexual duality which constitutes humanity, and we must begin with a central factor in biblical interpretation: context. Paul's statements about sexuality and women are especially prone to misinterpretation by ignoring the context in which they were uttered, and by trying to apply them literally to the very different situations of today.

In general, Paul's undeniable attitude of male superiority can be explained by his total background, not all of which was eradicated in his conversion to Christianity. Even though he recognized that "if any one is in Christ, he is a new creation" (2 Cor. 5:17), it is simply unrealistic to suppose that Paul, the "Pharisee and son of Pharisees," did not retain many of the deeply ingrained beliefs of his past, especially since these were still supported by virtually all of those with whom he had contact (although, significantly, not by Jesus himself, as we have seen). We might wish that Paul had transcended his heritage more fully on this particular issue, but both Scripture (cf., e.g., 1 Cor. 11:8–9) and tradition (cf. 1 Cor. 14:34) constrained him. His attitude was, in short, the incorrigible result of a long tradition supported by his contemporary context.

Furthermore, since Paul's primary concern was spreading the gospel, he was only incidentally concerned with social issues and avoided any effort to begin a social revolt that would have detracted from, or discredited, the gospel of Christ that he preached. He would therefore likely have accepted most of the social views of his tradition and culture, as is clearly evidenced in his attitude toward slavery. Helmut Thielicke asserts that "the unreflective way in which Paul . . . takes over contemporary ordinances as theologically valid could be for a–*horribile dictu!*–'modern theologian' a grave fault";[19] and we must

18. *Women in Church and Society* (Nashville: Abingdon Press, 1972), p. 69.
19. *The Ethics of Sex*, John W. Doberstein, trans. (New York: Harper & Row, 1964), p. 305. The author refers specifically to slavery and to 1 Cor. 11:5, 13.

conclude that the failure of theologians since Paul to realize that he did thus utilize the common views of his day is an equally grave fault. Paul perhaps can be forgiven as a man of simpler times, but theologians today who continue to appeal to Paul as authoritative on this issue lack such a justification for their action.

It is important to note that there is clearly a dialectic in Paul's thought, already indicated by the fact that he could commend women for their work in the church at the same time that he forbade them from participation in some of its major activities and urged their submission. This same tension shows up in Colossians, where Paul cannot rest content with a simple command for wives to be subordinate—he must immediately counter this with an injunction for husbands to love their wives and not treat them harshly (vv. 18–19).

Paul's apparent struggle shows up most clearly, though, in 1 Corinthians 11. In verses 7–8, he makes a strong case for the inherent inferiority of woman based on the Genesis creation accounts; then, in verses 11–12, almost as if he had second thoughts, he asserts that "in the Lord" (an important phrase for Paul in this context) man and woman are interdependent. This is not to say that Paul is self-contradictory, but that the dialectical nature of his thought on this issue should be recognized before any conclusions are drawn one way or the other.

Given, then, Paul's limited and dialectical perspective on the question of the place of woman, what contribution can his thought make to our concern? We have already seen how Paul stresses mutuality in the man-woman relationship vis-à-vis sexual rights within marriage, a theme that is continued in the Pauline-influenced letter to the Ephesians (5:21). The Colossians *Haustafel* (3:18–4:1) again states this mutuality: Wives are urged to be subject to their husbands (v. 18), but husbands are immediately commanded to love their wives and to treat them well (v. 19). The husband-wife relationship is thus given new meaning by the actions that are to be carried out "as is fitting in the Lord" (v. 18).[20] Also, as we have just seen, in 1 Corinthians 11:11–12

20. The mutuality is further emphasized by Paul's injunctions in vv. 12–13 to "put on" compassion, kindness, patience, forgiveness, and the like, culminating in the command, "above all these put on love, which binds everything together in perfect harmony" (v. 14). He clearly had this idea in mind when he wrote four verses later about the husband-wife relationship. It is also significant that immediately before these injunctions there is a direct echo of Gal. 3:28, though here without specific mention of the sexual distinction (v. 11).

Paul again claims that "in the Lord" there is a mutual interdependence of man and woman.

This mutuality "in the Lord" leads to the interpretation (1 Cor. 11:3 and also of Eph. 5:22–25) presented by Schnackenburg: The parallel of Christ as head of the husband, and the husband as head of the wife, indicates that the dominance and subordination which is commanded is to be understood not legalistically but *analogically*. Christ exemplified the servant, not the master, and his authority was love, not coercion. Similarly, the husband's headship is not that of a ruthless master but of a loving servant—for the reverence shown the husband by the wife there is returned a sustaining love.[21]

It is yet another aspect of Paul's description of the man-woman relationship "in the Lord," however, that provides the real key to an understanding of his contribution in this area of our inquiry. As we have seen, Paul held to his culture's view of the inequality of the sexes and the inherent inferiority of woman. For him, this was apparently a fact brought about by the original order of creation (1 Cor. 11:7–8); and since this order still prevailed, the social inequality remained intact. But, as W. D. Davies points out, Paul's eschatological emphasis caused him to understand as the church's goal the inauguration of eschatological unity, of which the original unity of creation is the prototype (1 Cor. 11:11–12). That is, the church is to recreate unity between man and man (woman) as well as between man and God by reordering the relationships that were disordered by the Fall.[22]

"In the Lord," then, the *social* hierarchy no longer determines the woman's value since social structures pertain to the order of creation and not to the order of salvation, even though for Paul, as for Jesus, the former foreshadows the latter. Nevertheless, until the *eschaton*, decent order must be upheld in the churches, and thus Paul issued his ordinances of 1 Corinthians 11 and 14 which we have examined. When he spoke about everyday practical affairs, the inherited social patterns held. But, when he spoke "in the Lord"—who as the new Adam was already part of the "last things"—he stressed the mutuality and interdependence of God's original and final design.

---

21. *Moral Teaching*, p. 252.
22. "The Relevance of the Moral Teaching of the Early Church," in E. Earle Ellis and Max Wilcox, eds., *Neotestamentica et Semitica: Studies in Honour of Matthew Black* (Edinburgh: T. & T. Clark, 1969), p. 45.

The classic statement of this position is of course Galatians 3:26–28, which is an excellent summary of the actualization of Christian faith in life; and there is no more fitting passage with which to conclude an examination of Paul's view of women. As we have seen, his attitude was somewhat paradoxical: On the one hand, his tradition, supported by a literalistic reference to the J creation account, led him to see women as definitely inferior to men; on the other hand, he felt very strongly the demands of Christian love.

Indeed, Paul often struggled with his Jewish background as it was confronted and challenged by his Christian faith, and his tradition sometimes won, especially on specific points such as dress in church and social roles. But when it really mattered, in his general theological statements, the power and truth of the gospel which he preached came through. Thus he was able to write Galatians 3:26–28, whose words are unfortunately so alien to man's egotistic propensities that they were *not* the ones chosen to interpret Paul's position and to guide the church and society:

> For in Christ Jesus you are all sons of God, through faith. For as many of you as were baptized into Christ have put on Christ. There is neither Jew nor Greek, there is neither slave nor free, there is neither male nor female; for you are all one in Christ Jesus.

In the church's inauguration of eschatological unity, then, sexual as well as cultural and economic differences (perhaps in Paul's view the "archetypal" distinctions among humans epitomizing all others) are to be transcended. But it is clear that Paul did not imply any disparagement of sexuality by this statement since it is characteristically a *religious* affirmation. That is, it refers to the equal dignity of all before God and the equal availability of salvation to all. It does not necessarily have any "ontological" significance: it implies the elimination of structural differences between male and female no more than it decrees the freeing of slaves (cf. Philemon and 1 Cor. 7:21).

As Schnackenburg points out, even in communion with Christ, Paul does not contend that natural conditions and distinctions are eliminated, but only that they lose their power to sunder the unity of God's creation and divide humanity into conflicting factions. In Paul's religious perspective, the question finally is not one of natural characteristics of the sexes (a particular view of which we have seen that, as a

Jew, he held), but only of their equal worth before God through belief in the saving work of Jesus Christ.[23]   And if in God's eyes, according to Paul, all humans are of equal worth, can the church as the body of Christ strive for anything less?

23. *Moral Teaching*, p. 252.   Robin Scroggs has put the point well by saying that although *distinctions* remain, the *values* and *roles* based on those distinctions no longer obtain.   See "Paul and the Eschatological Woman: Revisited," *Journal of the American Academy of Religion*, XLII (September, 1974), 533.

5

Science:
The Biological Basis of Human Sexuality

For all the insights the Bible can offer us into the nature of human sexuality, few people today are willing to accept the biblical statements as the final word on the topic. We do not live in the biblical era, and we have developed new methods for acquiring knowledge and new canons for evaluating the knowledge we already possess. Although the human race has long had a practical knowledge of sex, we are only now beginning to gain a theoretical understanding of the truly complex mechanisms that make the "simple act" possible. Even so, our knowledge of the biological workings of sexuality is infinitely greater than that which was available to those of biblical times. Before we can attempt our constructive effort of presenting a contemporary Christian view of human sexuality, therefore, it is necessary to examine some of the most pertinent and significant findings in this area. Otherwise we may be guilty (and we would certainly be accused) of basing our reconstruction on archaic, inaccurate information that has been invalidated and superseded by recent research.

This examination will be facilitated if we note at the outset that human reproduction by means of copulation between two different mating types—male and female—places man firmly in the line of evolutionary relationship to other animals, especially the mammals. It is not necessary to examine the wealth of ethological data directly relevant to sexuality which have appeared recently. One ought, however, be aware that much of the current knowledge of human sexual functioning derives at least presumptively from such observations and from the experiments of animal behaviorists and other researchers, and we shall make use of some of their findings later in this chapter. There is much to be gained, then, from comparisons with lower animals. Indeed, much of what we now know about human sexuality would have been unattainable had we not been able to experiment with animals and make cautious application of the results to man.

These contributions of ethology and comparative physiology notwithstanding, an extremely important caveat, especially for our purposes, must be introduced: Whatever the value of comparisons of humans with other animals, certain factors (to be discussed shortly) render easy conclusions dangerous, if not impossible. One must be very careful to maintain clearly the distinction between verifiable data and extrapolated speculation, a distinction unfortunately all too often overlooked in much popular writing on the topic. Jacob Bronowski sounds a needed warning when he reminds us that what is really "natural" to man has to be what is *specific* to him. Thus, attempts to apply general ethological accounts of animal behavior to man are invalid, and the effort of ethologists to find "universals" in animal behavior is distorted from its proper goal if it is used "as a prescription for what is 'natural' in human conduct."[1]

With this reservation clearly before us, we can now reaffirm man's continuity with the rest of creation, a fact which has long been recognized by classical Judeo-Christian theology and more recently (since Darwin) by Western science. Given this biological continuity, there is little reason to suppose that the basic *biological* processes which occur in the human species are significantly different from those of infrahuman species, especially the higher primates. The observation of differences between species, just as of differences *within* a species, does not negate the assumption of biological continuity. Thus, only if we take seriously studies of sexual behavior in all species can we claim to have considered all the evidence available for evaluating our own sexuality.

If there is considerable biological continuity between human sexuality and that of infrahuman animals, however, most authorities agree that a major difference exists in the psychological realm. Indeed, this is such a quantitative difference that it becomes qualitative and, in many instances, offsets or even overrides the biological similarities. Interestingly, those scientists who recognize this difference (and most do, at least implicitly) almost uniformly attribute it to a human capacity long celebrated in theology, viz., man's self-awareness. And this self-awareness is made possible by a particular evolutionary development in the human species.

1. "Technology and Culture in Evolution," *The American Scholar,* 41 (Spring, 1972), p. 20.

The highly evolved cortex of the human brain (the neocortex) distinguishes the human from all other creatures in terms of the ability to rationalize, conceptualize, and symbolize one's relative position, actions, and their consequences within one's environment. Hence, the human confronts the world with a unique capacity to "plan" a given action based upon accumulated memory of past experiences, knowledge of present exigencies, and anticipation of future needs and events. Furthermore, the human can evaluate the consequences of actions and store this information symbolically (either internally or, perhaps more importantly, externally) for future reference.

The significance of this capacity for our concerns is readily apparent. Clellan Ford and Frank Beach, for instance, after stressing the highly developed state of the cerebral cortex in man (90% of adult brain mass), suggest that the evolutionary decrease in "instinctive," hormonally controlled behavior (especially sexual) coincides with an increase in cortical control over such activities. They conclude that, since all complex human behavior depends greatly on the cortex, "it is automatically open to modification through the influences of previous experience."[2] This position is merely a restatement in biological language of the point made three centuries ago by Blaise Pascal in his celebrated statement, "Man is but a reed . . . ; but he is a thinking reed. . . . All our dignity consists, then, in thought."[3]

It is not my purpose to argue for the validity of self-awareness as a major difference between man and other animals. Nor is such an effort necessary since so many scientific writers acknowledge the distinction, albeit in different language perhaps. I deny to animals neither awareness (they are surely not Cartesian "machines") nor the ability to modify their behavior through learning. I merely claim that they lack *self*-awareness. As Teilhard de Chardin says in *The Phenomenon of Man*, "Admittedly the animal knows. *But it cannot know that it knows*: that is quite certain."[4] All animals copulate (if they are to survive as a species), but only man *thinks*, writes, and talks

2. *Patterns of Sexual Behavior*, Harper Colophon Books (New York: Harper & Row, 1951), pp. 254–55.
3. *Pensées: Thoughts on Religion and Other Subjects*, William F. Trotter, trans., H. S. Thayer and Elisabeth B. Thayer, eds. (New York: Washington Square Press, Inc., 1965), No. 347.
4. Bernard Wall, trans., Harper Torchbooks (New York: Harper & Brothers Publishers, 1959), p. 165.

about it, and worries about the problems he experiences with it—and all of his sexual problems (excluding a few fairly easily identified ones of physiological origin) are caused by this very ability to think about what it is he is doing. This situation seems to indicate that man's sexuality is not *merely* physical or only an instinct to be gratified whenever felt and with whomever one happens to be at the moment.

Indeed, this fact is tacitly acknowledged by Ford and Beach in a biological context (see above, p. 81), as well as by most of the writers who affirm human continuity with other animals. Because the human species is not controlled sexually by estrous or menstrual cycles, as even the infrahuman primates are to a large extent, sexuality for humans becomes a matter of thought, of will, and especially of imagination. In addition to the undeniably physical dimension of human sexuality, there thus appears to be an important psychological dimension.

Since unbridled sexual indulgence traditionally has been thought to be "animalistic," showing man's side as a "brute," the generally accepted conclusion I want to adopt from the various disciplines of animal research may at first seem surprising: To put it simply, the human being is "hypersexual." Robert S. DeRopp puts it quite unequivocally, saying that "by the standards of other mammals man is excessively, almost insanely sexual."[5] Desmond Morris's statement of the case probably has had wider public exposure: "Clearly, the naked ape is the sexiest primate alive."[6] That this assessment is accurate is illustrated in part by the duration and variety of human foreplay, the large number of positions used for coitus, and the continual receptivity of the female and readiness of the male for copulation.

Given the highly developed state of the human brain and our relative freedom in sexual activity from endocrine timing, it is not surprising that few, if any, researchers today feel that human sexuality can be described adequately in biological terms alone. Biological knowledge, though necessary for a full understanding, is not sufficient without a consideration of the psychological and social dimensions of sexuality. Before we can consider some of the non-biological aspects of human sexuality, however, a firm foundation must be gained in the

5. *Sex Energy: The Sexual Force in Man and Animals* (New York: Delacorte Press, 1969), p. 34.
6. *The Naked Ape* (New York: Dell Publishing Co., Inc., 1967), p. 53.

biological factors that not only provide the apparatus for human sexual expression but also greatly influence one's understanding of oneself as a sexual being. This is the primary purpose of the rest of this chapter.

The Developmental Variables

For most people, gender determination (which for many is virtually equivalent to what "sexuality" means) is basically a matter of a cursory observation of the external genitals. Indeed, two leading researchers in the field state: "Dimorphism of response on the basis of the shape of the sex organs is one of the most universal and pervasive aspects of human social interaction."[7] It may be surprising, therefore, that in his widely accepted schema for sexual differentiation, John Money lists no less than *seven* interdependent variables that determine one's sex. Arranged in the order in which they are most likely to make their major contribution to sexual differentiation, the variables are as follows: (1) genetic or chromosomal sex; (2) gonadal sex; (3) fetal hormonal sex; (4) internal morphologic sex; (5) external morphologic sex; (6) hypothalamic sex; and (7) sex of assignment and rearing.[8]

Genetic or Chromosomal Sex

The facts about genetic or chromosomal sex are familiar to every high school biology student. One of the most important biological discoveries of the twentieth century has been that life is transmitted through a self-replicating code, deoxyribonucleic acid (DNA), which is contained in the nuclei of cells. Individual genes, which pass hereditary elements from parent to offspring, are segments of DNA molecules.[9] In organisms that reproduce sexually, sexual activity

7. John Money and Anke A. Ehrhardt, *Man & Woman, Boy & Girl* (Baltimore: Johns Hopkins University Press, 1972), p. 12; hereafter cited as *Man & Woman*.
8. Money, *Sex Errors of the Body: Dilemmas, Education, Counseling* (Baltimore: Johns Hopkins University Press, 1968), p. 11.
9. Good summaries of molecular biology may be found in W. Hayes, "Molecular Genetics: An Introductory Background," and in M. R. Pollock, "Molecular Genetics: Short-term Applications and Long-term Possibilities," both in Watson Fuller, ed., *The Biological Revolution: Social Good or Social Evil?*, Anchor Books (Garden City: Doubleday & Company, Inc., 1972), pp. 47–94. A more thorough, but more difficult, discussion of the same material may be found in Philip Handler, ed., *Biology and the Future of Man* (New York: Oxford University Press, 1970), Chaps. 2 and 3, pp. 7–130.

serves to combine information contained in the genes of two individuals of the same species. Indeed, the term *sex* often is defined
biologically simply as an exchange and combination of genetic material. The normal human cell contains forty-six chromosomes, which
are the threadlike structures in the cell nucleus that contain the genes,
which are in turn, as just mentioned, the hereditary factors composed
of DNA that are transmitted from parent to offspring. All the cells of
the human body are *diploid* (i.e., they contain the full complement of
twenty-three pairs of chromosomes) with the exception of the sex
cells or *gametes* (the "marrying" couple of sperm and egg). By a
process of reductive division different from that of any other human
cell, these *haploid* cells alone contain only twenty-three chromosomes,
one of which determines sex. The ovum contains only an X chromosome (so called because of its shape), whereas the sperm contains
either an X or a Y chromosome and is thus the gender-determining
gamete.

When the sperm and ovum unite in fertilization, each contributes its
genetic material to the creation of the first complete, diploid cell of
the human being. If a sperm containing an X chromosome (a gyno-
sperm) fertilizes the ovum, the sex-determining pair of chromosomes
is XX. Assuming that everything proceeds normally, differentiation of
a female will occur. If fertilization is accomplished by a sperm containing a Y chromosome (an androsperm), the combination XY
indicates normal differentiation as a male. The exact mechanism by
which the chromosomal combination initiates this differentiation is as
yet unexplained, except that in some way it determines whether the
undifferentiated gonad will develop as a testis or an ovary. Surprisingly, after serving this function, the sex chromosomes play no known
role in the further determination of sex.

Gonadal Sex

It appears, then, that in one sense the second variable, gonadal sex,
is perhaps the most crucial; that is, once the *basic* determination is
accomplished by the sex-determining chromosomes, it becomes the
task of the fetal gonads (ovaries or testes) to carry out the actual
sexual differentiation. The interdependence among the variables,
however, is illustrated by the fact that this differentiation is actually
accomplished by means of the next variable, hormonal sex.

In gonadal differentiation, a pattern is set that recurs later in the differentiation of both the internal and, with a slight variation, the external morphologic sex: The anlagen (i.e., the primitive tissues from which more developed structures differentiate) for both male and female gonads at first exist side by side, after which one proliferates and differentiates, while the other regresses and atrophies. For about the first six weeks after conception there is no apparent embryonic sexual differentiation, with the same sets of ducts developing in both. Then, if the embryo bears the XY genetic code, the testes begin to develop from a primitive structure, originally potential testes *or* ovaries. In this case, the medulla, or core portion, of the primordial gonad proliferates while the cortex, or outer layer, regresses. If the genetic code is XX, the opposite differentiation occurs, though not beginning until the twelfth prenatal week, when ovaries differentiate from the cortex. This difference in time of differentiation has crucial effects, as we shall see shortly.

As was mentioned above, the way in which the X and Y chromosomes initiate gonadal differentiation is not yet known; the assumption, however, is that the XY chromosome pair stimulates the production of an "inductor substance" from the primitive gonadal medulla. This substance, probably an androgen (male hormone), causes the development of a few cells which in turn begin to secrete more androgen necessary to bring about further proliferation of the gonads.[10]

Hormonal Sex

As the gonads differentiate, they begin to secrete the all-important hormones (which, incidentally, are also produced by the cortex of the adrenal glands). In an interesting reversal of the Genesis account of man's creation, in which the male was created first, and something *taken from him* to create the female, the basic plan embryologically is to create a female unless something specifically causes a male to differentiate. "Stated in nontechnical terms, the . . . familiar embryonic and fetal rule is that something *must be added* to produce a male."[11] Thus, in the absence of any gonads or hormones, the fetus differentiates autonomously as a female, but it can *only* differentiate as a male in the presence of "something added," viz., the secretions of the fetal

10. *Man & Woman*, p. 2.
11. *Ibid.*, p. 147.

testes. The direction of sexual differentiation, therefore, is dependent at this stage solely upon the presence or absence of the male hormone, without which female gonadal differentiation occurs even without specifically female hormones.

It is interesting to note that in oviparous (egg-bearing) animals, such as birds and reptiles, the situation is reversed: The basic propensity is to form a male unless the female hormone estrogen is present. This fact helps us to understand why the mammalian pattern is as it is. Because mammals are viviparous (i.e., bear their young alive after a relatively long intrauterine period), the fetus is constantly bathed in maternal (female) hormones through the placental blood supply. Thus, if female hormones were the "trigger substance," all mammals would be born female! But, with male development dependent only on the presence of the male hormone, those fetuses which produce this hormone can differentiate as male despite constant exposure to high levels of female hormones.

It is important to remember, of course, that in the normal human being the gonads (and adrenal glands) secrete *both* male and female sex hormones, in amounts and proportions varying greatly among individuals. Hormonal differences between the sexes, therefore, are not absolute but a matter of degree, and thus, it is impossible to determine biological maleness or femaleness by hormone assay alone. Biologically speaking, then, the primary prenatal role of the sex hormones is to effect development of the body in accord with genetic sex, and thus to provide later reproductive capability.

Internal Morphologic Sex

We have seen that the sex-determining chromosomes cause either ovaries or testes to develop. These, in turn, secrete hormones that influence the next variable in sexual differentiation, i.e., the structure of the internal reproductive organs. Here is seen again the importance of the temporal priority of testicular differentiation because, in the absence of secretions from the testes, the female internal structure differentiates. Since the internal genital structure begins its development in the seventh week after conception, and since the testicular hormones are necessary if this differentiation is to take place as male, the testes must have differentiated earlier. The female structures, in contrast, differentiate "automatically," even without ovarian hormones.

Until this internal differentiation occurs, the human embryo contains the primordia of both the male and the female genital ducts, being in a sense hermaphroditic, or even androgynous. When the female develops, the *mullerian ducts* function as the anlagen for the uterus, fallopian tubes, and upper vagina, and the *wolffian ducts* undergo involution. If the development is male, the mullerian ducts atrophy and the wolffian ducts become the vas deferens, seminal vesicles, and ejaculatory ducts. Again, the presence of the secretions of the fetal testes is the key, although here too the exact mechanism is not presently known.

As we have seen, something must be added to make a male, and in this case, there are two additions. First, there seems to be an unidentified chemical substance which functions unilaterally, causing the mullerian duct adjacent to each testis to atrophy, and which is called simply the "mullerian-inhibiting substance." Second, there is testosterone, the male sex hormone, which at first has a localized, unilateral (bilateral if one testis is missing) effect, causing the wolffian duct to proliferate; later testosterone circulates through the blood stream to the anlagen of the external genitals and initiates their differentiation as male.[12]

External Morphologic Sex

Unlike the plan of development of the gonads and internal genital structure, in which the primordial anlagen for both male and female are initially present side by side, the external genitals differentiate from the *same* primordia. This, the final step in the embryonic development of sexual morphology, is again under the control of the hormones produced by the testes. Here also the basic principle holds: In the presence of male hormones, differentiation as a male takes place; in their absence, differentiation as a female occurs with no specific female factor necessary.

As might be expected, there is a "critical period" in fetal life when the presence of testicular hormones is mandatory if the single anlage of the external genitalia is to differentiate as male. This period is "marvelously short" in humans, comprising a few days late in the third month after conception. If male hormones are absent during

12. *Ibid.*, pp. 40–42, 7.

this time, differentiation as a female occurs, a condition which is there-after hormonally irreversible.[13]   Because the differentiation of the external genital structures begins from exactly the same primordia, perhaps here, more than in any other variable, is there possibility for error and mishap in the usual plan of development.   Such errors are at least certainly more visible.

Hypothalamic Sex

As for the next variable, hypothalamic or "brain" sex, the evidence is admittedly slight since it is based mostly on animal research, which yields results that are problematic in direct application to human development.   Nevertheless, some findings are generally accepted, and their importance to an understanding of human sexuality from a biological perspective warrants a summary of the main points.   Some early endocrine research suggested the pituitary as the site of some type of sexual differentiation, but further experiments showed that it is actually the brain itself that is subject to this effect.

Once again, the active agent appears to be the male hormone, and the principle followed is the now familiar one that something must be added to make a male.   In the opinion of G. W. Harris and W. C. Young, who were early proponents of the new theory, "the brain of a mammal was essentially female until a certain stage of develop-ment. . . .   If testosterone was absent at this stage, the brain would remain female; if testosterone was present, the brain would develop male characteristics."[14]   This organization of the brain occurs at about the same time in human fetal development that the testes' hormones trigger the differentiation of male sexual morphology.   The masculinization of cells appears to occur in the small part of the brain called the *hypothalamus,* phylogenetically the oldest part of the mam-malian brain.

Affecting primarily self-preservation and continuation of the species, the hypothalamus maintains stability in the body's internal environ-ment through control of the autonomic functions, such as respiration, pulse, and blood pressure.   The hypothalamus is also the segment of the brain "most immediately involved in the regulation of sexual behavior,

13. *Ibid.,* pp. 43–45.
14. Seymour Levine, "Sex Differences in the Brain." *Scientific American* (April, 1966), 86.

most immediately sensitive to sex hormones, and most directly involved in regulating the activity of the endocrine system," this last through its control of the pituitary gland which, among its various functions, controls the production of gonadal hormones.[15] The hypothalamus, therefore, serves as "a gate or funnel for eroticism and mating behavior,"[16] and the nature of this behavior (i.e., as male or female) is profoundly and permanently determined by the presence or absence of male hormone during the critical period. At the present time the precise mechanism is unknown, though there is evidence that the effect on the brain is not to stimulate certain nuclei but to remove chemical blocks so as to allow transmission of impulses from one cell to another.[17] However this differentiation occurs, Corinne Hutt aptly observes that "this single fact, that *some part of the brain is characteristically different in males and females*, is one of the most significant findings in neuroendocrinology."[18]

When Robert Stoller wrote *Sex and Gender* (1968), he discussed the "very provocative thesis" that sexually dimorphic central nervous system subsystems exist for the regulation of sexual behavior. At that time, however, he commented that there was no *histological* evidence (i.e., observed differences in the actual tissues of male and female brains) for such subsystems, though "the experiments to date seem to demand such an explanation."[19] More recently, such evidence has begun to appear, and one study may be mentioned briefly. In 1971, Geoffrey Raisman and Pauline M. Field presented an "anatomical demonstration of sexual dimorphism" in the nerve connections of the preoptic area of rats. Although the preoptic area is not the hypothalamus, the two are closely connected, and the preoptic area plays an essential role in hormonal regulation in the adult rat, thus influencing sexual behavior. As Raisman and Field admit, anatomical sexual dimorphism in part of the brain is not proof of a direct relationship to sexually differentiated functions in the realm of sexual behavior. But,

15. Handler, ed., *Biology and the Future of Man*, p. 405.
16. Money and Ehrhardt, *Man & Woman*, p. 238.
17. Frank A. Beach, "Experimental Studies of Mating Behavior in Animals," in John Money, ed., *Sex Research: New Developments* (New York: Holt, Rinehart and Winston, 1965), p. 127.
18. *Males and Females* (Baltimore: Penguin Books, 1972), p. 34.
19. *Sex and Gender: On the Development of Masculinity and Femininity* (New York: Science House, 1968), p. 6.

occurring as it does in an area shown to be directly involved in sexual responses, it is "persuasive circumstantial evidence."[20]

It appears, then, that testicular androgens play a dual role: In the fetal period their action is organizational, involving not only sexual morphology but also the neural tissues that will mediate sexual behavior in the mature organism and will determine whether, other factors being favorable, its behavior will be male or female in character; in adulthood, the male hormones serve to activate that behavior.[21] It should be noted also that, given the importance of the hypothalamus for regulating so much essential behavior and the close interconnections among various parts of the brain, it hardly seems likely that other aspects of behavior besides the sexual (in the sense of "reproductive") would not in some way be affected by the differentiation of the hypothalamus according to sex.

Although the danger of applying results in animal experiments to man must be constantly borne in mind, W. C. Young and his co-workers maintain that the findings presented in this section raise the possibility of the concept of predetermined psychosexuality in contrast to a psychosexual "neutrality" at birth which is yet to be filled in by experience. Young *et al.* recognize that the experiences of their test animals are important and that experience and learning play an even larger role in human psychosexual development. Nevertheless, they conclude that relationships between many behavioral states and hormonal effects on the developing fetus and the adult may exist. Thus the possibility that "typical and deviant behaviors have a physiologic as well as a psychologic basis may no longer be excluded."[22]

In our discussion of the six developmental variables that have been considered so far, we have been able to remain exclusively within the realm of biological research. We have seen that the human embryo, starting from what are for practical purposes the same sexual structures, differentiates through a series of steps into a male or female.

20. "Sexual Dimorphism in the Preoptic Area of the Rat," *Science*, 173 (August 20, 1971), 731–33.

21. Experimental evidence strongly indicates that the male hormone (androgen) is the libido hormone for both men and women. That it is the *male* hormone, however, which induces sexual desire has no known effect upon the *nature* of one's erotic impulses, i.e., whether one is aroused by males or females and according to the different patterns typically found in men and women.

22. William C. Young, Robert W. Goy, and Charles H. Phoenix, "Hormones and Sexual Behavior," *Science*, 143 (January 17, 1964), 216–17.

The whole process is apparently triggered by either an XX or an XY chromosome pattern. This pattern causes hormones to be produced which lead to the development of internal and external sexual organs and which seem to have some effect on the brain itself. But these strictly biological data do not exhaust the factors which constitute human sexuality, and biology, for all its important contributions to man's knowledge of himself through a clearer understanding of the physical bases of sexuality, cannot provide a final answer to the question of what it means to be a sexual being. A consideration of the seventh variable in Money's schema will confirm the validity of this judgment.

6

The "Nature-Nurture" Debate:
Contributions from Anthropology and Psychology

The first half of the seventh and final variable proposed by Money can be briefly discussed. Sex of assignment, quite simply, refers to the determination of the sex of the newborn infant, almost always by examination of the external genitalia by the attending physician, and subsequent entry upon the birth certificate of this finding. However, when we turn to an examination of the second half of the variable—sex of rearing—the situation becomes very complicated. This complexity is perhaps not surprising when one realizes that the first six variables are shared to some extent by all mammals, and that it is only when we consider the seventh variable that we enter the predominantly human realm. Indeed, with the first six variables we have discussed only *mammal* sexuality, not *human* sexuality, since the latter is distinguished primarily by the importance of the seventh variable.

Thus, it can be said that the first six variables define the terms *male* and *female* in a biological sense, but what is important for us is that the seventh variable is apparently essential in the definition of *masculine* and *feminine*. That is, animals are male or female, but hardly "masculine" or "feminine." These latter terms simply do not apply, even when we describe behavior: The behavior patterns of animals are male and female, *not* masculine and feminine. Our common usage reflects the inappropriateness of imparting to an animal either masculinity or femininity: However clearly a dog may be demonstrating his gender, we would never say that he is a "masculine" dog, but always that he is a "male" dog. Thus it appears that "masculine-feminine" is a cultural (and therefore *human*) distinction, which is largely determined by the seventh variable, i.e., the way in which the child is reared.

It is also worth noting in this context that "masculinity" and "femininity" denote characteristics that have little to do with one's ability to engage in coitus or reproduction. This fact leads to the conclusion, consonant with the point just made about animals, that *male* and *female* describe the results of the first six variables (i.e., the preparation of the individual for a role in the propagation of the species), but that *masculine* and *feminine* describe considerably different (and predominantly human) characteristics that are the result of the seventh variable.

"Sex of rearing," therefore, introduces us to the long-standing "nature-nurture" debate, which has regained momentum recently under the impetus of both scientific research such as that reported above and, perhaps more significantly, of the women's movement for equality. The literature on this topic is voluminous, and the main point of my effort is not to present a comprehensive review, much less to argue for one side or the other. Nevertheless, when one is attempting to understand human sexuality, some effort to come to grips with the different aspects of the controversy is mandatory because our view of what it means to be sexual beings has always been governed by the basic dichotomy of "male" and "female," along with some opinion about what each term means. I shall therefore discuss several basic concepts, first summarizing the major contribution of the biological research reported in Chapter 5 and then presenting some of the significant findings of cross-cultural anthropology and of psychology.

Contributions from Biology: A Brief Review

Hypothalamic Sex

The major contribution of biological science to the discussion has already been presented in some detail in relation to the variable of hypothalamic sex. In brief summary, the presence or absence of fetal androgen during the critical period causes the hypothalamus (that part of the brain most directly associated with sexual behavior) to differentiate as male or female; the exact nature and mechanism of the differentiation are still not clear, although there is some evidence that it may involve actual anatomical changes. Differences in behavior of males and females therefore appear to be mediated not only by different proportions of hormones but also by differences in the parts of the central nervous system that produce the behavior by responding to the hormones.

Those on the "nature" side of the debate can clearly gain comfort from these findings. This is especially obvious, for instance, when Young, Goy, and Phoenix claim that their research allows for the explanation of so-called masculine or feminine behavior "without postulating a psychosexual neutrality at birth and attributing the gender role and sexual orientation solely to the individual's life experiences while growing up." They feel that the early organizational action of the hormones on the brain establishes "much of the sex-related behavior which is a part of the masculinity or femininity of an individual but which is not related directly to the reproductive processes."[1]

This theoretical assertion has received very interesting clinical corroboration from a study of fifteen girls with adrenogenital syndrome which has been reported by Money and Ehrhardt. This syndrome results from the increased production of androgen by the fetal adrenal glands, leading to varying degrees of masculinization. All of the girls in this study apparently had been diagnosed early and given both cortisone treatment and corrective surgery. Eleven of the fifteen fetally androgenized girls claimed to be tomboys (a claim supported by their mothers and playmates), not as a transitory episode, but as a long-term way of life. This tomboyism manifested itself in several ways. There was a marked preference for rough, active outdoor games with high energy expenditure, often team games with a ball, though none of the girls was especially aggressive in terms of fighting. This preference led logically to a desire for practical clothes such as slacks and shorts rather than dresses.

These girls also showed less interest in hair styles, jewelry, and other adornments than did a matched control group of normal girls. The fetally androgenized girls preferred guns, cars, and trucks in play and they neglected dolls. As the girls grew up, this same pattern manifested itself as a lack of interest in infants and their care, including paid baby-sitting. One-third of the girls did not want to have children at all; the other two-thirds showed considerably less enthusiasm than the controls, all of whom "eagerly anticipated motherhood." For most of the controls, therefore, marriage was their prime goal for the future. Most of the adrenogenital girls, however, either desired to have a career in addition to being a housewife—seeing the two as equally important—or they subordinated marriage to a career. Con-

1. "Hormones and Sexual Behavior," 216, 217.

cordant with this preference, they were also later than their age mates in reaching the stage of dating and having boyfriends, though there is no evidence of lesbian tendencies in fetally androgenized girls.

These results clearly support the position of Young *et al.*, especially in light of the conclusion drawn by Money and Ehrhardt: The "most likely hypothesis to explain the various features of tomboyism in fetally masculinized genetic females is that their tomboyism is a sequel to a masculinizing effect on the fetal brain." The masculinization may affect pathways in the brain which control dominance assertion (leading to competitive energy expenditure) and which eventually mediate maternal behavior (causing a lack of interest in dolls and infants). Money and Ehrhardt claim a "noteworthy lack of masculinization" of those pathways that "mediate love and eroticism in response to a mating partner," and they feel that the crucial factor in this respect operates postnatally rather than prenatally. It will be important for subsequent discussion to note the investigators' final comment on this study: Such a large part of one's ultimate identity as male or female takes form postnatally "that prenatally determined traits or dispositions can be incorporated into the postnatally differentiated schema, whether it be masculine or feminine."[2]

Contributions from Anthropology

The Importance of Cross-Cultural Studies

If we now consider some of the cross-cultural material relevant to the nature-nurture controversy, we find an apparent swing in favor of the "nurture" side. There are, of course, a number of problems inherent in the studies (most caused by the very *subject* studied), and these must be recognized. In the first place, as Alfred Kinsey and his colleagues recognized, many anthropologists have been reluctant, because of their own cultural conditioning, to examine specific matters of sexual behavior. Furthermore, the societies studied have usually been preliterate, a situation which limits greatly the sources of information available. From general conversation, a few informants, and observations of public behavior, many valuable data have been gathered, but anthropologists readily admit the large gap that exists between the behavior recorded by such methods and that which actually occurs in private. The very insistence on privacy in sexual behavior, an almost universal aspect of human behavior, further limits

2. *Man & Woman*, p. 103; the entire study is reported on pp. 98–103.

research by direct observation, or even by detailed inquiry, because the demand for privacy often leads to elaborate taboos against discussions of sexual activity. At best, then, such studies illustrate the behavior of some members of a given culture but cannot necessarily be said to describe adequately patterns that are prevalent throughout it.[3]

Even with these and other shortcomings to which they are subject, cross-cultural studies are still valuable in a discussion of the nature-nurture debate, as well as in an attempt to understand human sexuality in general. We often tend to equate the particular behavior patterns of our own culture with "human nature," and it is crucial, especially in an area such as sexuality, that we realize that other human beings manage quite well even though their actions, attitudes, and concepts differ considerably from those which we experience daily.

Money and Ehrhardt, referring to cultures other than our own, state the point that I am making in a way which is worthy of quoting in its entirety because of the connection they draw with the biological data presented above:

> Their traditions of sexual-dimorphism of behavior, which differ so greatly from those of our own culture, must be acknowledged by the scientists of our own culture—acknowledged not as fortuitous behavioral quirks, sins, or pathologies but as manifestations of potentially universal human behavior. This must be taken into account before any theory can be satisfactorily formulated to explain human sexuality and sex differences, whether from the point of view of genetics, prenatal hormones, postnatal hormones, the prenatally programmed brain, or the postnatal brain programmed by way of contingency learning.[4]

The Work of Margaret Mead

It is neither possible nor necessary here to present in detail the results of the many cross-cultural studies of sexual behavior that have been published. It may be helpful, however, to offer a very brief sketch of the results of Margaret Mead's *Sex and Temperament in Three Primitive Societies* in order to indicate the type of findings often presented in such studies. *Sex and Temperament* is an examination of three primitive tribes within a 100-mile area of New Guinea: In one tribe, the mountain-dwelling Arapesh, both men and women

---

3. *Sexual Behavior in the Human Female*, Pocket Books (New York: Simon & Schuster, Inc., 1965), pp. 92–93.
4. *Man & Woman*, p. 135.

behave as our society traditionally has expected women to behave—in a mild, responsive, parental way; in a second tribe, the river-dwelling Mundugumor, the ideal for both sexes is closer to our stereotype of masculine behavior—aggressive, fierce, with little parental concern; in the third tribe, the lake-dwelling Tchambuli, the expectations of our culture are actually reversed—the woman is the dominant, unadorned, impersonal, managing partner, whereas the man is emotionally dependent, less responsible, and prone to gossip and concern about personal appearance.[5] Thus, in three geographically proximate tribes, we find two in which *our* cultural ideas for one sex are held by both, and one in which these ideals are reversed.

From her research, Mead concludes that the temperaments that we consider to belong to one sex are "mere variations of human temperament to which the members of either sex or both sexes may, with more or less success in the case of different individuals, be educated to approximate."[6] Contrary to the opinions of some of her critics, she does not claim that there are *no* sex differences, and she recognizes that all known societies treat sexual dimorphism as a differentiating factor of the same magnitude as difference in age, the other similar "universal."[7]

Indeed, in a warning appropriate to our time, Mead insists that the claim that there are no sex differences in a society in which they have always played an important role may have as subtle a standardizing effect on personality as the insistence that many such differences exist.[8] In sum, as different as various cultures are in patterning human sexual differentiation, "there are basic regularities that no known culture has yet been able to evade."[9] These regularities are excellently summarized by Money and Ehrhardt:

> In the final analysis, culturally prescribed (or prohibited) gender-dimorphic behavior stems from the phyletic verities of menstruation, impregnation, gestation, and lactation. These verities are procreative

5. *Sex and Temperament in Three Primitive Societies*, Mentor Books (New York: New American Library, 1935); hereafter cited as *Sex and Temperament*.
6. *Ibid.*, p. xvi.
7. "Cultural Determinants of Sexual Behavior," in W. C. Young, ed., *Sex and Internal Secretions* (third ed.; Baltimore: Williams & Williams Co., 1961), II, 1451.
8. *Sex and Temperament*, p. 229.
9. *Male and Female: A Study of the Sexes in a Changing World*, Laurel Edition (New York: Dell Publishing Co., Inc., 1949), p. 154.

imperatives, so to speak, in the design of any culture's definition of male and female roles, if that culture is to maintain its membership and survive.[10]

These basic biological realities notwithstanding, the major conclusion that Mead draws from her cross-cultural studies tends to support the "nurture" side of the debate. Since the temperamental attitudes that we view as either masculine or feminine can be totally reversed or forbidden to both sexes in other cultures, there is no longer any reason for considering such aspects of behavior to be determined by sex. Most of the traits we attribute to men or to women are, in Mead's opinion, no more necessarily linked to sex than are particular clothing or hair styles assigned to either sex at a given time. In short,

> we are forced to conclude that human nature is almost unbelievably malleable, responding accurately and contrastingly to contrasting cultural conditions. The differences between individuals who are members of different cultures, like the differences between individuals within a culture, are almost entirely to be laid to differences in conditioning, especially during early childhood, and the form of this conditioning is culturally determined. Standardized personality differences between the sexes are of this order, cultural creations to which each generation, male and female, is trained to conform.[11]

In other words, although the first six variables determine in which of two roles the child will be reared, it is the individual society that decides *what* those roles will mean, what their *content* will be. Support for this conclusion will be found as we turn now to some psychological considerations in the nature-nurture controversy.

Contributions from Psychology

The "Neutrality-at-Birth" Theory

Earlier, a clinical study reported by Money and Ehrhardt was used to support experimental evidence that prenatal hormonal influences may predispose the fetal brain to later masculine or feminine behavior. There is a certain irony in this because John Money (along with his colleagues John and Joan Hampson) is generally considered to be the chief proponent of the "nurture" side of the debate, an advocate of what has even been called the "neutrality-at-birth" theory. That we are here venturing into the psychological realm of the debate can be

10. *Man & Woman*, p. 145.
11. *Sex and Temperament*, pp. 205, 206.

readily seen in one of the clearest statements of the position for which Money is known. He states that masculinity or femininity of outlook is so fixed in the healthy human that it has always been considered to be set automatically, as for instance, by genes or hormones, independent of life experience. He feels, however, that his research now demands the conclusion "that erotic outlook and orientation is an autonomous psychologic phenomenon independent of genes and hormones and, moreover, a permanent and ineradicable one as well."[12]

The Hampsons align themselves with Money's view when they claim:

> the evidence militates too strongly against a theory of innate, preformed, and inherited behavioral imperatives, hormonal or otherwise. . . . Instead the evidence supports the view that psychologic sex is undifferentiated at birth, a sexual neutrality in the place of the Freudian bisexuality, and that the individual becomes differentiated as masculine or feminine, psychologically, in the course of the many experiences of growing up.[13]

The position taken by Money and the Hampsons, then, is basically that both self-awareness as male or female (gender identity) and overt behavior, displayed as a result of that awareness (gender role), are *learned* through social interaction after birth and can be largely, or even totally, independent of chromosomes, gonads, hormones, morphology of sexual organs, or any other common determinant of sex.

What is the "evidence" for this bold position which constitutes what one critic calls "a formal challenge to the classical concept of human sexuality"?[14] It is impossible to provide a detailed account of the many case studies presented by Money and the Hampsons. A word about their methodology, with a few examples, will, however, indicate the basis for their position. Much of their clinical evidence derives from the study of various human sexual anomalies which may be defined generally as examples of hermaphroditism. This condition includes not only those rare individuals in whom relatively complete male and female sexual organs both exist ("true hermaphrodites"),

12. "Sex Hormones and Other Variables in Human Eroticism," in Young, ed., *Sex and Internal Secretions,* II, 1397.
13. "The Ontogenesis of Sexual Behavior in Man," in Young, ed., *Sex and Internal Secretions,* II, 1428, 1413.
14. Milton Diamond, "A Critical Evaluation of the Ontogeny of Human Sexual Behavior," *The Quarterly Review of Biology,* 40 (June, 1965), 148; hereafter cited as "Ontogeny of Sexual Behavior."

but more commonly those in whom variance occurs between the pre-
dominant external genital morphology and one or more of the following variables: chromosomes, gonads, hormones, and internal genital
morphology ("pseudohermaphrodites").

One of the most interesting cases cited in support of the neutrality-
at-birth position concerns a normal male infant whose entire penis was
destroyed in an accident during circumcision. He was reassigned as
a girl at seventeen months and underwent corrective genital surgery.
The parents were counseled as to the best way to handle the child's
rearing, and after a six-year follow-up period since surgery, Money
and Ehrhardt report the following results: The child shows a clear
preference for dresses and dolls, pride in her long hair and neatness, a
desire to help her mother with the housework, and the expectation of
marriage and motherhood some day. She does display many tom-
boyish traits, but she is still, as her mother puts it, "so feminine. I've
never seen a little girl so neat and tidy." Interestingly, she has an
identical twin brother, who is "very masculine" in all his preferences
and interests, ruling out the possibility of undue parental influence
toward femininity.[15]

Money and Ehrhardt also report several cases of matched pairs of
pseudohermaphrodites with the same diagnosis at birth, but different
sex of rearing. A brief look at one of these pairs will indicate the
nature of this evidence. Both children are genetic females with
adrenogenital syndrome, born with ambiguous genitals. One was
assigned as a girl, surgically corrected, and spending an unremarkable
childhood. She displayed the tomboyism typical of the syndrome, but
still "everything about this girl was very attractively feminine."

The second child was assigned as a boy, corrected surgically, and
masculinized at puberty with androgen therapy. Academically he
was an underachiever, and he spent his time with a group of quasi-
delinquents, though he was not overly aggressive. Significantly, his
romantic feelings and advances were totally limited to girls. Money
and Ehrhardt conclude that these matched-pair studies "demonstrate
conclusively how heavily weighted is the contribution of the postnatal
phase of gender-identity differentiation"; beginning with the same
clay, "one may fashion a god or goddess."[16]

Finally, Hampson and Hampson present some more quantifiable

15. *Man & Woman*, pp. 118–23.
16. *Ibid.*, p. 152; the case presented here is reported on pp. 154–56.

data that can be briefly summarized. They studied more than 110 hermaphroditic individuals and reached the following conclusions: Of the 20 reared in the sex discordant with their chromosomal sex, every one had a gender identity in accord with sex of rearing (i.e., XYs reared as girls considered themselves to be female and XXs reared as boys saw themselves as male). Concerning the other variables of sexual differentiation, the results are as follows (the denominator of the fraction is the total number of subjects in which the given variable was discordant with the sex of assignment and rearing; the numerator represents those individuals whose gender identity was nonetheless in accord with sex of rearing): gonadal sex—27/30; hormonal sex—26/31; internal sexual morphology—22/25; external sexual morphology—23/25. Overall, of the 131 comparisons made, there were only 7 inconsistencies (5%) between gender identity and sex of rearing (3 of 7 appear for more than one variable). Based on evidence such as this, the Hampsons' conclusion is not surprising: "Thus, in the place of the theory of an innate, constitutional psychologic bisexuality . . . we must substitute a concept of psychologic sexual neutrality in humans at birth."[17]

Criticisms of Psychosexual Neutrality

Needless to say, such a position, even when supported by considerable evidence, is likely to evoke a flood of criticism, not the least of which concerns the interpretation of the evidence itself. Some critics are content to dismiss the theory with a passing remark, as Mary Jane Sherfey does in a footnote; referring to the Hampson statement quoted just above, she says: "Since 'neutrality' means here what it seems to mean [of neither sex], I cannot see that the theory helps simply because it is not true."[18] Perhaps the most thorough critique of the Money-Hampson position (though not without its own biases of interpretation) is the essay by Milton Diamond cited earlier. Since some of these concerns will be important for our later attempt to reach a contemporary understanding of human sexuality, let us consider briefly here several of the most significant difficulties with the Money-Hampson hypothesis of sexual differentiation.

Diamond reports the results of a number of studies that seem to

17. "The Ontogenesis of Sexual Behavior in Man," 1406; the study summarized above is reported on 1408–13.
18. "The Evolution and Nature of Female Sexuality in Relation to Psychoanalytic Theory," *Journal of the American Psychoanalytic Association*, 14 (January, 1966), 42.

indicate (again subject to one's interpretive biases) that the male and female nervous systems exhibit differential levels of response to environmental stimuli. This is certainly not unreasonable to assume in light of the recent research into the organizational effects of gonadal hormones on the fetal brain. Some of the differences Diamond mentions include threshold to electrical shock (lower in females as early as the first three days of life), olfactory acuity (greater in women *and* varying with hormone level), response to erotic stimuli (more visual in men), sensitivity to tactile stimuli (greater in women), blockbuilding (more symmetrical and compact designs by boys), and interpretation of Rorschach forms (many variances).

It can of course be argued (as it has been) that these differences are learned, but the nature of some of the variances, as well as of the tests used to measure them, seems to permit the judgment that at least some of them are present from birth.[19] The import of this is that if males and females *are* differentially responsive to external stimuli through physiological differences in the nervous system, then postnatal experience may be determinative (as Money and the Hampsons claim), though not in quite the way they claim it is. That is, one's gender identity may well be primarily determined by experiences after birth, but there is a strong possibility that the "identical" experience would have a quite different effect on the psychosexual differentiation of a male or female—he or she would receive the stimulus differently through differentially reactive nervous systems, certainly a *biological* influence on the experiential one.

This same kind of criticism can be made on a slightly different level. Again, granting the extreme importance of postnatal experiences in the differentiation of gender identity, it nevertheless must be borne in mind that these experiences are to a large extent determined by one's *biological* sex, as determined by chromosomes, gonads, hormones, internal sexual organs, and especially external genitals. For example, the reactions of parents, siblings, and friends vary greatly from a child with genitals of a male to one with those of a female. Money and Ehrhardt are quite aware of "a whole pattern of dimorphism of rearing girls and boys with respect to genitalia, sex and reproduction."[20]

19. "Ontogeny of Sexual Behavior," 163–64. The second half of Corinne Hutt's *Males and Females* consists of a detailed presentation of these and other differences along with the clinical and experimental evidence which supports them.
20. *Man & Woman*, p. 120.

Here, again, is a clear example of some of the child's most crucial post-natal experiences being strongly conditioned by the physical manifestations of sex with which he or she is born. It is reasonable to assume also that the effect of one's rearing will be enhanced if that rearing is congruent with one's biological sexuality.

Furthermore, paralleling this "external" influence is a more "internal" one: Just as the reactions of others to the child are largely determined by his or her bodily sex, so are the child's own responses, beginning in earliest infancy with the first awareness of its own body.[21] In other words, a high correlation exists between biology and experience: Biology functions as the *independent* variable, and postnatal experience as the *dependent* variable, in the equation that will eventually issue in gender identity. Biological development, in that it precedes experience, thus not only serves as the substrate to be molded by experience but can be said, to a large extent, to set limits upon what much of that experience will be.

That others, as well as the child itself, react to the bodily sex of the child may indicate one of the dangers inherent in basing one's hypotheses solely upon studies of anomalous individuals in which the physical manifestations of sex are questionable, as Money and the Hampsons do. It may well be that, simply because the ordinary biological determinants of gender are equivocal in these cases, the psychological and social elements in psychosexual differentiation are called upon to play a much more central role than they normally would have to play. Indeed, this observation can be extended into a more general judgment upon the methodology used by these investigators to reach their conclusions.

It would appear that Money and his colleagues have called on their data to support a weightier conclusion than they can in fact bear. It is one thing, and perfectly legitimate in light of the presented evidence, to say that humans—when confronted with situations of equivocal sexual identity—*can* differentiate a gender identity and role discordant with their biological sex. It is something else, and probably not substantiated by the evidence, to extrapolate from these hermaphroditic experiences the conclusion that *all* humans, including those

---

21. For an interesting treatment of this point from a "neo-Freudian" perspective, see Warren J. Gadpaille, *The Cycles of Sex*, Lucy Freeman, ed. (New York: Charles Scribner's Sons, 1975), especially Chapter 2, "All-Encompassing Influences during the First Eighteen Months."

of normal sexual biology, *do* acquire their gender identity as a socio-cultural accretion with practically no influence from the inherent limitations which biology imposes. In short, because it can happen that way in some cases does not mean that it does happen that way in every case, or even in most cases.

This ability to "overcome" one's biology may rather be a good example of the generally accepted finding of animal behaviorists that in man, evolution has allowed a great deal of flexibility of behavior with respect to hormones (and other physical determinants of sex). Thus, sexual behavior in man becomes much more modifiable by learning, a fact usually attributed primarily to the highly evolved state of the human brain and man's release from rigid hormonal regulation.

The unusual occurrence, then, would be if certain humans could *not* overcome various anomalous physical determinants of sex in order to differentiate a healthy and acceptable gender identity. Again, however, this does not imply, on the basis of currently available evidence, that the human ability to modify behavior, which in lower species is determined by biology, renders the individual completely free from any sort of "prenatally determined pattern and mechanism of sexual behavior."[22] Money and Ehrhardt succinctly recognize the minimum that can be said here: "Nature herself supplies the basic irreducible elements of sex difference . . . : women can menstruate, gestate, and lactate, and men cannot."[23]

Conclusion

We have now reviewed some of the major recent contributions to the "nature-nurture" controversy from three different perspectives: biology; cross-cultural anthropology; psychology. We are not, however, in a position to rule in favor of one side or the other, nor is that our task. In fact—the overenthusiastic claims of some proponents of each position notwithstanding—any sort of definitive answer is probably still far in the future. Until researchers can experiment with human infants in the same controlled setting in which they work with animals, the question of whether, or to what extent, sexual differences are innate or learned will remain open to debate—and fortunately no one has yet considered settling the issue to be *that* important! Given this lack of planned experiments designed specifically to solve the

22. Diamond, "Ontogeny of Sexual Behavior," 166.
23. *Man & Woman*, p. 13.

unanswered questions, what can be said about the nature-nurture debate at this time?

In the first place, as one reads the writings of those most involved, there is a strong impression that this is really a "misplaced debate." Diamond, for instance, concludes that the "proper interpretation of human sexual behavior must not stumble on debate of nature versus nurture. Undoubtedly both are significantly involved."[24] Money and Ehrhardt are even more explicit in their approbation of modern genetic theory's avoidance of the "antiquated dichotomies" of nature-nurture, genetic-environmental, innate-acquired, biological-psychological, and instinctive-learned; and they insist that the "basic proposition should be not a dichotomization of genetics and environment, but their interaction."[25]

Moreover, the Hampsons contend that investigators are beginning to abandon the "fruitless effort" to discover the proportion of environmental or hereditary contribution to a particular pattern of behavior.[26] The concern is rather, as I have tried to show, *how* the various factors operate in determining behavior. After all, when one examines human sexual behavior, the separation of genetics and environment is analogous to the separation of hydrogen and oxygen as far as their respective contributions to the properties of water.[27] There seems to be simply no way of quantifying the relative inputs of the different variables, of assigning a "percentage of contribution."

The best conclusion to be reached at this stage appears to be the one which most investigators have reached, namely, that both elements are necessary and crucial. On the one side, Money and Ehrhardt admit that their evidence "shows rather conclusively that there are in human beings some gender-dimorphic behavior differences based on antenatal hormonal history." Nevertheless, they stress that "these differences do not automatically dictate or totally preordain" later gender differentiation, but that postnatal events exercise a weighty influence on the way in which "prenatal determinants or dispositions will be incorporated into the final gender-dimorphic behavioral product."[28]

On the other side, Diamond maintains that, instead of adopting the

24. "Ontogeny of Sexual Behavior," 167.
25. *Man & Woman,* p. 1.
26. "The Ontogenesis of Sexual Behavior in Man," 1403.
27. Diamond, "Ontogeny of Sexual Behavior," 158.
28. *Man & Woman,* p. 117.

neutrality-at-birth theory, one should admit that in sexuality as in other areas "the human being is extremely flexible and his behavior is a composite of prenatal and postnatal influences with the postnatal factors superimposed on a definite inherent sexuality."[29]   A careful reading of the two positions shows that they are saying virtually the same thing but emphasizing opposite poles.   In sum, what seems clear at this time is that there are biological determinants operative in sexuality but that these can be greatly modified by the postnatal experiences of the individual.

29. "Ontogeny of Sexual Behavior," 169.

Reconstruction:
A Dialectical View of Human Sexuality

The task that now confronts us is to bring together, into a useful Christian understanding of human sexuality, such information as has been obtained by two rather different approaches, and considered from very different perspectives. These may even appear to be mutually exclusive. Indeed, in the past these two views often have been in conflict and have had very little that was constructive to say to each other. Although a history of science, and especially of its split with theology, is clearly beyond the scope of this chapter, several comments are necessary in order to lay the foundation for the reconstruction which I shall propose.

Generally speaking, one of the chief characteristics of the modern (i.e., post-Reformation) period has been specialization. No longer is one discipline able to answer all of man's questions about himself, his environment, his origin. Rapidly expanding human experience and knowledge have demanded ever greater division of subject matter and consequent specialization. One of the most significant manifestations of this departmentalism is methodological: Whereas theology begins with God, and explains all natural phenomena by reference to this "highest" principle, science starts with the individual experiences and observations of humans, and seeks to find regularities in them that provide their explanation. Thus "spiritual" concerns have increasingly become the province of theology, and science has concurrently devoted itself to understanding the "material," observable world.

Theology, beginning with its "highest" category, deals with the "lower" categories in the most suitable way that is consistent with that "highest" principle. Science, on the other hand, has as its goal the explanation of everything by the "lowest" category that can account for it. This approach is necessary for science in order to assure that each explanation is valid: Progress in science (i.e., more adequate and universally acceptable explanations of phenomena) depends upon the refusal to appeal to each "higher" category until it is satisfactorily proved that the "lower" categories cannot explain the phenomenon being observed.[1]

Theology, with its ultimate explanation always at hand, is often impatient with (and threatened by) the determination of science to find more proximate causes. Science, with its goal of explanation by the lowest category, finds theology's approach from the other end peripheral and perhaps even obstructionistic in the quest for true knowledge. Theology generally counts finally on revelation for its truth, whereas science depends upon observation and experimentation. These differences in the two approaches, radical as they are, were evident in the information presented in previous chapters.

More specifically, a great deal of our current trouble in understanding human sexuality stems from the period in which science and theology were beginning to go their separate ways. In fact, the rise of modern science itself was greatly facilitated by the same pivotal event of that period which has contributed to the current misunderstanding of sexuality, namely, the presentation by René Descartes of his dualistic philosophy. In barest outline, Descartes proposed that all reality is divided into two realms: *res extensa,* the world of bodies characterized by extension and rigid adherence to precise mathematical laws; and *res cogitans,* the world of unextended, thinking, spiritual substance which is independent of the first realm. Since living bodies are extended, they must be part of the *res extensa:* Animals are machines or automata, totally determined by physical laws, and the same judgment applies to human bodies, at least insofar as our bodies function largely automatically and without conscious attention.[2]

On this predicate, it follows that theology was given the realm of the spirit, of mind, while science claimed for itself exclusive concern with the material world and the body, which could be observed and

1. William Temple, *Nature, Man and God* (London: Macmillan & Co. Ltd, 1964), pp. 45, 47; hereafter cited as *NMG.*
2. René Descartes, *The Philosophical Works of Descartes,* Elizabeth S. Haldane and G. R. T. Ross, trans. (2 vols.; Cambridge: Cambridge University Press, 1931). Concise, helpful summaries of the philosophy of Descartes may be found in Frederick Copleston, *A History of Philosophy,* Vol. IV: *Descartes to Leibniz* (Garden City: Image Books, 1960), pp. 74–160; and in E. A. Burtt, *The Metaphysical Foundations of Modern Science,* Anchor Books (Rev. ed.; Garden City: Doubleday & Company, Inc., 1954), pp. 105–24.

measured. Since the two realms are autonomous and independent of each other, it is not surprising that theology and science, both of which have operated largely from a Cartesian foundation since the sixteenth century, have had little constructive interaction in an area such as sexuality, in which the interrelationship between body and spirit is so intimate.

Descartes's dualistic view of reality, in conjunction with the method that he used to reach it—universal doubt, in which the only thing unable to be doubted is the doubting *self*—led to a dualistic view of man: The individual is composed of two substances, an extended machine for a body and an independent, unextended mind. This view was not itself new—dualistic epistemologies and anthropologies existed long before Descartes proposed his—but it caused Descartes considerable difficulty: How does interaction occur between the two separate substances that comprise the human being? In fact, Descartes gave the problem little attention, merely asserting that interaction does occur and situating this interaction in the "pineal gland."

Thus, Descartes's dualism faced the same problem on the level of interaction *within* man that it did on the level of interaction between man and his environment: Subject and object, observer and observed—which are always connected in human experience—were separated. Epistemological problems, with which philosophy has struggled ever since, were raised, and the developing scientific mind was given an approach to the observation and description of reality that has contributed to the difficulties which we face today in understanding and coming to terms with our sexuality.

A cardinal methodological axiom of science is precisely this role as "detached observer," objectively scrutinizing and recording. Since the body is only a machine (albeit an amazingly complex one), it is proper procedure for the scientific mind to observe it only from without, especially since Cartesian dualism suggests that there is an unbridgeable gap between the observing mind and the observed matter. When sexuality is conceived to be a bodily function (as, of course, it manifestly is), then it is a legitimate object for such detached observation, evaluation, and perhaps even experimentation.

The dualistic view of man, which was thrust upon the rising scientific mind by Descartes, has thus resulted in a naturalistic, biological reductionism, a major component of which is the attempt to explain human action in general—and sexuality in particular—by reference to biological or even physical processes alone. Our sexuality is then, on these terms, something we can observe and discuss rationally; it is even something we can manipulate and alter in order to cause it to perform its functions "better" or more efficiently, functions which are taken to be obvious and transparent. The "machine" continues to yield more and more of its secrets to the ever-inquisitive observers.

It is ironic that this dualistic view of man, which led science to view the material world as the only reality, found natural affinity and mutual support in some of the views of what should have been its most obvious antagonist, Christian theology. Although dualism of this sort is not found in either the Old or the New Testament, Gnosticism and Manichaeanism—under the influence of Greek thought—denied the goodness of the material world, and hence of the human body, in exaltation of the spiritual. Neither of these movements gained orthodox status, but their influence (primarily through Augustine, and especially with respect to sexuality) opened the way for theology's acquiescence in the bifurcation of reality into matter (the province of science) and spirit (the concern of theology) which gained considerable support in the thought of Descartes.

Thus, there is pressure from two sides to maintain the separation of spirit and matter, of mind and body, which makes comprehension of our nature as sexual beings so difficult. On the one hand, science must insist that phenomena of the physical world be explained by physical categories and principles, without reference to spiritual or supernatural causes. Rigidly adhered to, this approach places spirit in an expendable position as far as the understanding of reality is concerned; and spirit's relation to and interaction with the material world becomes as problematic as it was for Descartes.

On the other hand, religion has tended to try to keep the spiritual as free as possible from contamination by the material, which has been seen as inferior and dangerous: Insofar as one's spiritual life is seen as morally determined, there is little room for consideration of physical forces or biochemical activities as relevant at all. Thus again spirit has nothing to do with matter, and spiritual exaltation has its counterpart paradoxically in either rigid asceticism or unbridled libertinism.[3]

Each of these views—the "scientific" and the "religious"—I maintain,

3. Temple, *NMG*, pp. 485–86.

is untrue both to the biblical understanding of reality and human nature and to the everyday experience of our existence as human beings; nor is either approach ultimately able to answer our questions about ourselves, especially about our sexuality. Let us look, then, at a way—based on *both* of the approaches presented in previous chapters— in which the dualistic split may be overcome. After a brief outline of the basic approach, we can consider more carefully some of the manifestations that our dualistic preconceptions have taken with respect to our understanding of human sexuality, and we can suggest ways in which these misconceptions might be corrected.

Let me stress that I am not attempting a "harmonization" of science and religion: I am only making an effort, in the one particular area of sexuality, to show that the two approaches do have something to say and contribute to each other. As Temple points out, truth is unitary, and the seeking of truth by religion and by science should converge. Thus, he concludes, truth is best served, not by doing science "religiously" or religion "scientifically," but by listening with open minds to what both have to say about the subject under consideration.[4]

The Dialectical View

The approach that I propose for overcoming the dualistic sundering of mind from body, of self from sexuality, may perhaps best be characterized by the word "dialectical." The thought of William Temple— one of the most profound, though neglected, Christian thinkers of this century—provides a very useful foundation for the approach which I shall take. Temple conceived reality as a series of strata, in which each higher stratum requires the lower for its actualization, with such utilization also being the only means by which the lower realizes its own "fullness of being."[5] The strata that he considers important are Matter, Life, Mind, and Spirit, which, in this context, may be considered to be separate entities or various modes of action and response.[6]

Elsewhere he points out that the ranking of the levels one above another is of course not spatial but logical,[7] though such ordering has

4. *Ibid.*, p. 474.
5. *Ibid.*, pp. 474–75.
6. *Christus Veritas* (London: Macmillan & Co Ltd, 1949), p. 4; hereafter cited as *CV*.
7. *Christianity in Thought and Practice* (New York: Morehouse Publishing Co., 1936), p. 54.

a definite basis in reality. That is, without matter—without the physical body to be alive—life has no reality in our experience. Yet, matter only reveals what it can be when life possesses and indwells it. In the same way life, which is absolutely necessary for the emergence of mind, only reaches its full potential when mind (which is primarily characterized by its seeking the means to reach a fixed end presented to it as good by its natural appetites and desires) comes to work through it. Finally, the potential of mind, without which spirit has no vehicle of operation, is actualized only when it is directed by spirit, whose identifying characteristic is the ability not only to choose means to given ends but also to distinguish among various ends by reference to some higher standard.[8] Temple summarizes his basic position in this way:

> Life is unknown apart from living organisms, which are Matter informed by Life. Mind is unknown except in reasoning, living organisms. Spirit is unknown except in conscientious, reasoning, living organisms. Whether the higher grades can exist apart, there seems to be no means of deciding; in our experience they never do.[9]

Several comments are in order before considering the applicability of this schema to our topic. First, Temple admits and even stresses that the strata just described, if taken singly, are only abstractions: "Reality is a continuous whole within which the mind of each individual finds itself."[10] Thus, the apparent discontinuity, which at first seems to support the dualistic separation of body and spirit we have argued against, is seen in fact to be a legitimate heuristic principle: "Our inherited habit of thinking by means of supposed Real Kinds makes difficult for us the intellectual appreciation of continuity of growth, however eager the intellect may be to trace continuity in the world wherever it can."[11]

Indeed, a cardinal element in Temple's entire philosophical system is a radical denial of any discontinuity between mind and matter (or "spirit" and "body"). Or, to put it the other way around, he strongly affirms the evolution of mind from matter in that mind first appears as consciousness of processes that were active in the material world before

8. *NMG*, p. 475. Although Temple does not generally include it in his numerous discussions of the grades of reality, the next grade, which apparently supplies this "higher standard," is God.

9. *CV*, p. 6.

10. *Ibid.*, p. 5.

11. *NMG*, p. 114.

mind appeared: Matter is irreducible to a state of mind, just as mind is irreducible to any combination of matter.[12]   Thus there is an inseparable dialectical interrelationship and interaction between mind and matter.

Second, Temple is aware that his schematization of reality is open to misinterpretation, which results from either one of two preoccupations. Beginning at the lower end of the scale, on the one hand, there is no doubt about the reality of matter as the necessary basis for life, mind, and spirit; but, there is the danger that these higher strata will be believed to contain nothing of reality that is not observable in the material world.   In our case, this is the biological reductionism that tries to understand human sexuality completely as a "natural function" which can be explained by reference to physical processes alone.

On the other hand, if one stresses unduly the actuality of the spiritual, the equally necessary and valuable actuality of the material may be denied.[13]   This spiritualistic approach is, of course, the one that has dominated the Christian church's interpretation of sexuality, which has been considered to be an ugly manifestation of human "fleshly" existence and a major obstacle to the attainment of true spirituality. Temple's resolution of this potentially destructive dialectic illustrates his refusal to accept the matter-spirit dichotomy and contributes to our attempt to devise a Christian understanding of human sexuality:

> For as it is true that matter is the necessary condition for the actuality of life and this also of spirit, so also is it true that, in our experience at least, spirit arises within and as part of an organism which is also material, and expresses its spirituality, not by ignoring matter but by controlling it.[14]

The Biological-Bodily Aspect of Human Sexuality

The implication of this view of reality for our attempt to understand sexuality is clear: There is an inescapable dialectic between mind and body, self and sexuality. It is undeniable that whatever sexuality is, it is bodily, and much damage has been wrought by failures or refusals to recognize and grant this fact. Science has made us aware that we are part of the material world and that an understanding of ourselves

12. See, e.g., *NMG*, pp. 111–12, 139, 217–18.
13. *Ibid.*, p. 475.
14. *.Ibid.*, p. 477, in italics in the original.

requires that we come to terms with the material aspect of reality.
The material has thus become considerably more important in human
self-understanding, from the theological perspective no less than from
the scientific. Simply put, human beings *are* matter like the rest of
the reality we experience daily, and thus, the material cannot be simply that which we observe from without—we are *within* it literally
and we must acknowledge that fact.

Chapter 5 showed the basic biological nature of human sexuality,
with the six variables it shares with all animal sexuality. Our sexuality is something objective, governed by biological, chemical, perhaps
even physical laws, and, as a bodily function, it can be studied by the
methods and procedures of science. Furthermore, as Maurice Merleau-
Ponty reminds us, it must be stressed that it is only through one's
body that one understands other people (and oneself), just as it is
through one's body that one perceives objects. This means that
"there is interfusion between sexuality and existence, which means
that existence permeates sexuality and *vice versa.*"[15]

Thus, we can do very much what we want in our imaginations, but
our *bodies* remain the only concrete channel for gaining experience
of the world (the raw material for our reflection) and for giving life
to our thoughts and fantasies. In short, our bodies are the only means
we have of expressing our self-awareness, of expressing our*selves*.
Merleau-Ponty provides an excellent summary of the principle I have
presented and, at the same time, indicates the way in which it extri-
cates us from the dilemma into which Descartes pushed Western
thought:

> I am my body, at least to the extent that I possess experience, and yet
> at the same time my body is as it were a "natural" subject, a provisional
> sketch of my total being. Thus *experience of one's own body runs
> counter to the reflective procedure which detaches subject and object
> from each other, and which gives us only the thought about the body,*
> or the body as an idea, and not the experience of the body or the body
> in reality.[16]

Furthermore, since "we" exist as bodies, and our bodies on the most
basic level define our sexuality as male or female, it seems that the
experience of oneself, of others, and of the world—as well as all reflec-

15. *Phenomenology of Perception*, Colin Smith, trans. (London: Routledge &
Kegan Paul, 1962), pp. vii, 186, 269.
16. *Ibid.*, pp. 198–99; italics added.

tion upon it—occurs as male and female experience and self-consciousness. It must be this way for the human race: We *are* male and
female, and we must be aware of ourselves and of others from one
of those two perspectives.

The Psychological-Spiritual Aspect of Human Sexuality

Implicit in what has just been said about the biological, bodily
nature of human sexuality, however, is the other aspect of the dialectic
I am proposing, namely that, although our sexuality *is* bodily, it is
also considerably *more* than that. If our earlier examination of biological research into sexuality demonstrated its undeniably somatic
nature, the presentation of a biblical view of sexuality indicated that
the comprehension of our nature as sexual beings is not exhausted by
biological description alone. Indeed, the scientific evidence corroborates this judgment: The importance accorded the seventh variable
(i.e., the role of learning in human sexuality) by the authorities cited
in Chapter 6 suggests that many scientists recognize that sexuality in
the human species includes more than genes, genitals, and hormones.

Biologically, this extra dimension of human sexuality can be attributed to our highly developed cerebral cortex and the greatly
reduced control of human sexuality by endocrine timing. These two
factors explain why learning has so much greater an effect on the
development and expression of sexuality in humans than in any other
species. In all other animals, there is a largely automatic regulation
of sexual activity, with a consequent ordering of the functions necessary for survival—eating, resting, copulating, rearing, and so forth.
With humans, however, these controls for the most part have been
lost. In the place of such controls, as the added element in *human*
sexuality, as Oswald Schwarz puts it, "we get the spirit, and with it
the freedom of decision over ourselves,"[17] a uniquely human capacity
which is comparable to Temple's Mind and Spirit.

What I am suggesting is that Temple's notion of the strata of
reality be applied to the dualism of mind and body which is our
legacy from Descartes, an application which results in a dialectical
understanding of human sexuality. Matter (or body) is clearly necessary to our sexuality; but the sexuality of human beings cannot be

17. *The Psychology of Sex*, Pelican Books (Baltimore: Penguin Books, 1949),
p. 29.

adequately described or explained, nor can it be properly expressed, without reference to some other category, which Temple calls Spirit. The lower strata find their true meaning only when utilized by the higher, but the higher cannot exist and actualize themselves apart from the lower. In our case, the body may be said to be "preconditional to, but not definitive of," human sexuality, just as biological existence is necessary for personal existence but not a sufficient description of it. The same principle may be expressed by saying that our sexuality is dependent upon bodily manifestation but not reducible to it. In short, what we are and who we are are inseparable, but to say what we are is not finally to say who we are.

We can affirm, then, what Temple calls the "organic principle," namely, that the unity of the organism as a whole predominates in such a way that every part is under the control of that unity.[18] That is to say, on the one hand, that the mind or personality cannot express itself without the body, and thus, that the action of the entire person is controlled by the necessary interaction of the elements comprising the unity. Expression of the personality, in this understanding, is limited by the capabilities of the body to express it.

On the other hand, the body is not a demonic entity that can function apart from the total reality that is the person, but the external manifestation—the means of expression visible to the self and to others—of that total unitary reality which is mind *and* body. Action is the bodily expression of the self's volition: "The two, though distinguishable, are inseparable; they are *organically* one."[19] Ian Barbour takes a very similar position with his view of man as a "many-leveled unity," a concept which he sees to be in line with both the biblical and the scientific perspectives:

> The highest level of man's total being may be represented by the concept of *the self*, conceived not as a separate entity but as the individual in his unified activity of thinking, willing, feeling, and acting. The self is described not in terms of static substances but of dynamic activities at various levels of organization and functioning.[20]

Practically speaking, this principle leads to the conclusion that the

18. *NMG*, p. 48.

19. *Ibid.*, p. 200.

20. *Issues in Science and Religion* (Englewood Cliffs: Prentice-Hall, Inc., 1966), p. 363.

problem with inappropriate sexual expression is not that the body functions apart from, or in contradiction to, the personality or self (which assumes an invalid dichotomy), but that the body, as the outward manifestation of the total reality that includes it, expresses and acts upon the *wrong* beliefs and goals.

This unitary but dialectical view of man is obviously very closely akin to the biblical understanding of man as a psychophysical unity which was presented in Chapter 1. That man is a psychophysical unity means that his "body" (or "flesh") and his "soul" (or "spirit") are not separate substances that only accidentally cohere; rather, they are interdependent elements which together comprise the human being, and without both of which man would not be human. Paul Ramsey says that "man is an embodied person in such a way that he *is* in important respects his body. He is the body of his soul no less than he is the soul (mind, will) of his body."[21] Instead of considering the soul to be the "real" person, and the body to be something which that person has, it is more accurate to say that man *is* body, that he is both an animated, "ensouled" body and an incarnate, "enfleshed" soul.

Indeed, the very conception of the body as an "instrument" to be used by the soul implies a fundamental separation between our true "inner" selves and our bodies. Instead, we must acknowledge and accept that which is self-evident, but all too often denied: Matter and life (i.e., one's body), informed by mind and spirit, are essential partners in all human endeavors, however base or however noble. And, as Robert Francoeur points out, this means that sex, which in the first instance is bodily, is something that we are, not something that we have: "Human sexuality is coextensive with human personality."[22]

There is, then, a dialectical interrelationship between body and mind, sexuality and self. The former is necessary for the expression of the latter, in which expression it finds its true meaning. This necessary interdependence, however, should not lead us to assume that the relationship is one of radical equality: There is a hierarchy, as was implied in the earlier presentation of the strata of reality. Body and mind are not two equal elements which comprise the human being.

21. *Fabricated Man: The Ethics of Genetic Control*, A Yale Fastback (New Haven: Yale University Press, 1970), p. 87; hereafter cited as *Fabricated Man*.
22. *Utopian Motherhood: New Trends in Human Reproduction* (Garden City: Doubleday & Company, Inc., 1970), p. 241.

It is true that the body is necessary for the expression of the self, but the body only finds its real reason for existence as it is used by the personality for self-expression. Theologically speaking, as Christ is to the Church, so spirit is to the body (cf. Eph. 4:15–16; 5:23–24); the relationship, although each element is necessary, is not one of absolute mutuality. Harmon Smith points out that stressing the necessity of embodiment for personal existence "is not to say that who we are *as persons* is defined by either primary or exclusive reference to our bodies, or that our personhood does not transcend in important ways the limitations imposed by our bodies."[23]

This transcendence and ascendance of the spiritual over the material is a corollary of Temple's organic principle: "In so far as mind takes control of any organism it becomes its real principle of unity." If mind is present in an organism, it is present "as potentially, and always in some degree actually, the principle of unity of that through which it is active." Later, Temple says that mind is "immanent in the body which is organic to it," but that "mind transcends it; that is to say, the mind never receives full and exhaustive expression through the body," or in terms we have used, mind cannot be explained fully by reference to body.[24]

Purpose

The split between mind and body is overcome in Temple's thought because mind is seen to have arisen out of (and remains a constituent element in) the total process of reality that was going on before mind appeared: "There is no transition to be effected from Mind to Matter, because Mind, as we know it, *is* consciousness of an environment which is in one aspect material."[25] And we have just seen that mind, when it appears, becomes the true principle of unity of the organism of which it is a part. When mind thus becomes the unifying principle, when personality (which is always transcendent in relation to process) takes control of the process from which it arose, we have presented to us the chief characteristic of personality: *purpose*.

Purposive action illustrates mind transcendent in the body/mind unity for which I have been arguing. Such action differs from merely

23. *Ethics and the New Medicine* (Nashville: Abingdon Press, 1970), p. 113.
24. *NMG*, pp. 200–01, 282.
25. *Ibid.*, p. 218.

organic action and reaction "precisely in the fact that not only is it determined by the whole being of the agent, but that the agent is determining himself both at other times and in the very moment and act of choosing his course of conduct. Here there is manifestly a reference to something over and above the observable activity."[26] Man is not simply reacting to forces upon him; he is transcending the process of reality to the extent that his actions are guided by something which is not yet, that which is his goal and toward which his actions are purposive.

Rollo May, a practicing psychotherapist, further elucidates this point. In his excellent book, *Love and Will*, May discusses several dimensions of human existence which are roughly analogous to Temple's strata. The first (corresponding to Temple's "Life") is awareness, the level which is shared by humans and animals; it includes the experience of basic bodily needs and desires as well as of primary interactions with the environment. The second dimension ("Mind") is the progression from simple awareness to the form of awareness distinctive to human beings, namely, consciousness, or *self*-consciousness, though May considers this term redundant because consciousness necessarily involves an awareness of one's part in it.

When this dimension of consciousness has been reached, one sees oneself over against the world, as a discrete self; and the possibility of the next and third dimension—decision and responsibility ("Spirit")— arises for the first time:

> If I experience the fact that my wishes are not simply blind pushes toward someone or something, that *I* am the one who stands in this world where touch, nourishment, sexual pleasure, and relatedness may be possible between me and other persons, I can begin to see how I may do something about these wishes.

One becomes, as it were, able to see the world and other people in relation to oneself, and thus one's actions begin to be governed by a conscious knowledge of these relations and the possibility of fulfilling the obligations they place upon one. In May's terms, *intentionality*— or *will* or *purpose*—then enters the picture as a direct result of the rise of Mind or human self-awareness.[27]

26. *Ibid.*, p. 261.
27. *Love and Will* (New York: W. W. Norton & Company, Inc., 1969), pp. 262–67.

Imagination

Imagination was mentioned in Chapter 5 as a major factor in human sexuality, and it is here that we see much of the significance for human sexuality of man's capacity for self-awareness. Because he is aware of himself as a discrete self, man can abstract and symbolize beyond his immediate environment and experience. And for man, this symbolization is crucial for the mediation of sexuality. That is, humans can continue sexual stimulation and relationships although widely separated by time and space, a capability which is not available to other animals that are regulated by endocrine timing and that lack man's capacity for self-consciousness. The human can write love letters, read and write erotic literature, or simply remember last night's (or last week's or last year's) sexual encounter and anticipate the next one. This human capability for response to symbolic stimuli reduces considerably the need for a certain hormonal balance or even direct physical stimulation in order for the individual to become prepared for coitus—often only the proper words, or physiologically non-stimulating but "symbolic" actions, are all that is necessary, especially if the imaginations of the partners are active.

The importance of imagination (which includes both memory and anticipation) in human affairs is graphically demonstrated by Macbeth's famous statement which, though uttered in a context far removed from sexuality, is nonetheless equally applicable here because it illustrates one of the main reasons that human coitus is so different from that of other animals: "If it were done when 'tis done, then 'twere well it were done quickly" (I.vii). For man, though, because of his self-consciousness which issues in imagination, it (whether murder or sexual activity) is never "done when 'tis done," as the rest of *Macbeth* makes only too clear.

The crucial result of the importance of imagination is, quite simply, that the human potential of sex—what differentiates it from that of other animals—does not inhere in the physical act alone, the basics of which we share with most mammals. Rather, what gives human sexuality its distinctive character is our ability to reflect upon it, to experience it as something more than mere physical sensations. The meaning of the *act itself* is greatly influenced by what one *thinks* about it and *says* in relationship to it. Thus, whether a specific act of coitus is rape, seduction, mutual fulfillment of love, or something else depends not only upon the physical actions of the participants but also, and inextricably, upon the symbolizations with which they reflect upon it. This view is illustrated by and gains support from literature: There are the many individuals who have numerous sexual experiences but then discover a "true love" with whom their sexual activity takes on a new meaning which renders it qualitatively different from all their previous affairs. The difference is not in the *physical* act as such, but in the *total* act as a *personal* event.

Based on the foregoing discussions, the dialectical understanding of sexuality which I am proposing can be expressed briefly as follows: Our sexuality is undeniably bodily, but it is not merely bodily. On the one hand, we express our sexuality appropriately—i.e., we use our sexual organs to their intended and intentional purpose—when we (the whole self that includes those organs) are reflective and purposive in their use, and in so doing exhibit an activity that is *more* than simply somatic. On the other hand, scientific research reminds us that we can use our sexual organs purposively only within the limits defined and imposed by the organ systems themselves and, in this sense, boundaries to our purposive action are thus clearly set by our bodily-biological nature. A simple illustration will suffice to clarify the dialectic I have just described.

The penis can be used intentionally and purposively in carrying out the sexual function for which it is designed; indeed, for humans there must be some degree of reflection and intention for this purpose to be achieved since we are basically free from endocrine timing and purely "instinctive" sexual activity. Thus, one can intend loving union with another or brutal degradation of another's humanity, either of which is accomplished by the same objective and *physical* act of inserting the penis into the vagina. But the penis can *not* be used to write a love letter or to make an obscene phone call; the limits to the intentional, purposive use of the penis are set by the organ itself, by its biological capabilities, no matter what the individual may *want* to do with it.

Two Contemporary Misunderstandings

In the recognition of this dialectical interrelationship and interdependence lies the road to overcoming the body/mind dualism that has plagued Western thought, and thereby to understanding our existence as sexual beings. The failure to understand this dialectic—a failure which manifests itself in a denial of the validity of *both* components of the dialectic—has led to two major misunderstandings of human sexuality: An extreme *naturalism* which rejects the transcendent element in sexuality, and a radical *personalism* which denies the bodily aspect of sexuality.

Naturalism

Naturalism defines sexuality exclusively with reference to the body and the "natural" functions of its organs. The Roman Catholic Church is a prime illustration of the dangers of this approach. So far this Church has been unable to extricate itself from the trap of viewing procreation as the regulative principle of human sexual expression, because that is the objective purpose and function of the sexual organs. Reduced to its bodily, biological function, human sexuality serves to propagate the species. In official Roman Catholic thought, then, the purpose of sexual activity derives from what is supposed to be the obvious nature of the act of coitus itself.

This view was reaffirmed as recently as 1968 by Pope Paul VI in his encyclical *Humanae Vitae*. For example, he points out that "man does not have unlimited dominion over his body in general," nor does he, "with particular reason," have "such dominion over his generative faculties as such, because of their *intrinsic ordination* towards raising up life, of which God is the principle."[28] The practical application of this view is well known: After citing the "natural laws and rhythms" by which God wisely assured a separation between births, the Pope continues, "Nonetheless the Church, calling men back to the observance of the norms of the natural law, as interpreted by their constant doctrine, teaches that *each and every marriage act* . . . must remain open to the transmission of life."[29] Thus, one is mistaken to think "that a conjugal act which is deliberately made infecund and so is intrinsically dishonest could be made honest and right by the ensemble of a fecund conjugal life."[30] It must be granted that the Roman Catholic position does, of course, recognize the unitive aspect of marital sexual expression, but only as a secondary purpose which must remain subordinate

28. *Humanae Vitae*, Paragraph 13, in Floyd Anderson, ed., *A Newsman's View of the Birth Control Encyclical* (St. Meinrad, Ind.: Abbey Press, 1969), p. 63; italics added.
29. *Ibid.*, Paragraph 11, p. 62; italics added.
30. *Ibid.*, Paragraph 14, p. 64.

to the primary end of procreation. In such a naturalistic reduction the transcendent element of the dialectical tension between body and mind, as proposed in this book, has been largely overlooked.

Interestingly enough, this naturalistic reductionism is also illustrated by those sexual philosophies which deny importance to procreation and choose instead another objective, "natural" aspect of sexuality as its chief goal and purpose. A clear example of this view is the "healthy orgasm" philosophy of Albert Ellis, in which the most immediate and obvious *physical* element in sexual expression—the orgasm—is seen as the self-evident purpose of the action and therefore set up as its ultimate and sufficient goal.[31] Again, because of a preoccupation with the bodily aspect of sexuality, the spiritual and personal element is denied, with a resultant impoverishment of the total experience.

In the context of these two manifestations of naturalism, which result from a failure to maintain the tension in the dialectic that is sexuality, it is appropriate to consider briefly the oft-heard claim that human sexuality is a purely natural phenomenon, and that problems arise chiefly because we refuse to accept it as such. Illustrative of this view is the answer given by Don Sloan, M.D., to a question about "preferred coital position": "One cannot repeat too often William Masters' words: 'Sex is a natural function.' It only follows, then, that it is best achieved by 'doing what comes naturally.' "[32] But the dialectical view presented here suggests otherwise. Indeed, I have argued that there is much truth, if perhaps some overstatement also, to be found in Herbert Richardson's assertion that sex "is what is *least* natural about man. It is, rather, the dimension of human life where

31. Ellis has presented his view in a number of books; see especially *The Search for Sexual Enjoyment* (New York: Macfadden-Bartell, 1966).

32. "Answers to Questions," *Medical Aspects of Human Sexuality,* VII (January, 1973), 10. It is interesting to note that Dr. Masters and his coworker-wife Virginia Johnson have recently taken a large step beyond their popular image as proponents of a mechanistic, "natural" view of sexuality, which they gained during the research for their two best-sellers on sexual function and dysfunction—*Human Sexual Response* and *Human Sexual Inadequacy.* They have recently published a book (with Robert J. Levin) entitled *The Pleasure Bond: A New Look at Sexuality and Commitment* (Boston: Little, Brown and Company, 1974), in which they caution against "preoccupation with manipulative technique," which "turns persons into objects" (p. 238), and warn that "sex as a goal-oriented performance is the usual substitute when sex with emotional commitment either fails to develop or is deliberately avoided" (p. 94). In language that calls to mind the biblical notion of "one flesh," they assert that our sexuality provides the means (through touching) to bridge "the physical separateness from which no human being is spared, literally establishing a sense of solidarity between two individuals" (p. 238).

man's spirituality and freedom are manifest most clearly."[33] In short, human sexuality cannot be viewed in a completely natural way because it is considerably more than a simply "natural" entity.

It is true, of course, that human reproduction by means of sexual activity provides a link between our species and other animals, especially other mammals. Biologically speaking, man's continuity with the rest of nature is conclusively shown by tracing the lines of evolutionary development, one important element of which is the means of reproduction. Despite this biological proof for human similarity to other animals, however, there is also empirical evidence for man's distinction—if not actually for his uniqueness—from infrahuman animals. These data, primarily from the fields of ethology and comparative physiology, concern man's relative freedom from endocrine timing of sexual activity and his highly evolved cerebral cortex. These two facts make human sexual activity much less "instinctive" and much more dependent upon psychological as well as physical factors than is the sexual activity of other animals. Thus man's sexuality affords him uniqueness not only as an individual within his own species, but also as a species in relation to all other species.

Theodosius Dobzhansky thus grants that the normal development pattern of the human species clearly includes the sexual drive, but he reminds us that the explicit manifestations of this drive are greatly influenced by culture and, thus, are to some degree learned. He concludes that "even the consummatory sex act is not wholly instinctive."[34] For other animals copulation appears to be a virtually automatic act: If conditions are right, an almost unavoidable chain of events follows; for humans, there is simply no such compelling, uncontrollable "instinct." Anyone who has observed dogs copulating, for instance, cannot claim that *human* sexuality is purely "natural" and instinctive. Far from "animal passion" to be emulated, the copulatory behavior of such infrahuman animals is, so far as we can tell from observation, as passionless and mechanical as one can imagine. Again, it is clear that human sexuality is more than and also different from this kind of sexual activity.

Oswald Schwarz, a highly respected psychologist of sex, therefore criticizes attempts to prove the "naturalness" of sex by comparing the

33. *Nun, Witch, Playmate* (New York: Harper & Row, 1971), p. ix.
34. *Mankind Evolving*, pp. 215–16.

sexual behavior and the institutions of animals with those of man. The problem with this comparative proof, he says, is that under the comparisons "slumbers the idea that man is an animal plus 'something,' whatever that may be"; so if a human engages in unrestrained sexual behavior, we say that the animal in him has won out. But, according to Schwarz, this is both incorrect psychologically, and unfair to animals, because "animals are not defective men, but every species is perfect in itself." Thus "if a man loses or discards the additional 'something' that makes him human he does not become a perfect animal, but remains always an imperfect man."[35] It is appropriate to recall here Jacob Bronowski's point referred to earlier: What is truly "natural" for man is not what he *shares* with the other animals but precisely what is *unique* to the human species.

Thus the bromide that unrestrained sexual behavior by humans is "acting like an animal" is, as suggested in Chapter 5, both grossly inaccurate and unjust to other animals. Because of our freedom from endocrine timing, we have been able to spread sexual activity over a much larger span of time, effectively limited only by childbirth itself, which is a relatively infrequent occurrence for most human females. And because of our highly developed cerebral cortex, which permits reflection and thus imagination, we can normally perform the necessary physiological functions at any time, regardless of the body chemistry of either partner at the given moment. With this basically unlimited capacity for sexual stimulation and performance, man truly is "the sexiest primate alive." In fact, instead of "showing the animal" in man, our prodigious capacity for sexual activity is one of our most *human* characteristics.

Nevertheless, there is frequently an element of truth in even the most inaccurate cliché, and there is in this one. The truth in saying that unrestrained sexual behavior is acting like an animal lies not, however, as most people appear to take it, in a high *frequency* of sexual acts (i.e., their quantity), which we have just seen to be a peculiarly human possibility. Rather, the truth concerns the *nature* of the sexual acts (i.e., their quality): The saying recognizes that such behavior is usually in the context of momentary, transient encounters with little or no relationship between the participants. Here the specifically

35. *The Psychology of Sex,* p. 29.

human dimensions of sexuality (e.g., communication, partnership, and acquisition of knowledge of self and the other) are neglected, and then the actions really are suggestive of animal sexuality. Sexuality requires more than the proper functioning of the sexual organs if it is to be human (i.e., inter*personal*).

The dialectical view of human sexuality presented earlier supports the point just made: Human sexuality cannot be considered to be a purely biological phenomenon, or a purely bodily activity. The use one makes of the body, since the body *is* in a very real sense that person, must be considered, both in its function as an expression of the individual's self-concept and for the effects it may have upon the person. Paul Ramsey raises the issue plainly: "There are more ways to violate a human being, or to engage in self-violation, than to coerce man's free will or his rational consent. An individual's body, including his sexual nature, belongs to him, to his *humanum,* his personhood and self-identity."[36] In short, it is as possible to sin against one's body as it is to sin against one's soul. Neither violation is acceptable to the dialectical view of man that has been presented because, according to this concept, *both* are *equally* grave sins against the person, who is both body *and* soul.

Hence, one cannot engage in sexual activity for pleasure *alone,* solely for the gratification of the body, because the "body alone" does not exist. Any "physical" action necessarily involves the psyche, the "spirit," as well. And because of the special dialectical character of sexuality discussed above, here more than perhaps in any other sphere of human activity can attempts at isolated physical actions damage the individuals involved. Schwarz draws the pertinent conclusion which we would expect from our earlier discussion of the strata of reality when he says, "Human 'nature' is Nature permeated by spirit. Human sexuality is not a mere happening, it is a deed for which we are responsible, and if we meekly submit to the physical impulse, we incur guilt."[37]

Still within the context of the dialectical understanding of sexuality which I have proposed, the same point can be stated more positively. It is only in a deep relationship, in a situation of truly caring for

36. *Fabricated Man,* p. 87.
37. *The Psychology of Sex,* p. 22. For a biblical statement of man's responsibility in this area, see above, Chapter 2, "The Song of Songs."

another person—in short, in what is commonly called "love"—that we realize the potential of the psychophysical unity that is man. It is only here that sexuality and personality are fully integrated, and that sexual activity is a wholly appropriate vehicle of personhood: The body expresses the inner feelings and attitudes of the person; and the inner feelings motivate the body not only to full and proper expression but also to the greatest physical pleasure possible. The body truly becomes a *symbol* of the very self, expressing what can be expressed in no other way.

Schwarz agrees with this view and stresses that the potential of physical sexuality is fulfilled only when it is used to express personality. In fact, he thinks that speech is the best analogy to human sexuality because "we have the capacity to speak in order to express ourselves, our thoughts, emotions, intentions, etc." Thus for him, indiscriminate coitus is, in a felicitous phrase, "a kind of sexual loquacity,"[38] if not in fact, we might add, a "kind of lying" in that one makes the gesture of expressing something more than a biological relationship when nothing more exists.

May supports this view by his analysis of the *personal* nature of the male-female sexual relationship, which is shown by the act of coitus itself: Only humans copulate face to face, looking at each other. This posture represents, both symbolically and in terms of animal behavior, the ultimate vulnerability, the greatest exposure of one's very self. Indeed, for May this single fact "marks the emergence of man as a psychological creature: it is the shift from animal to man." Even monkeys—with whom man shares to some extent the seventh developmental variable otherwise reserved to him—"even monkeys mount from the rear." This change in love-making posture is so momentous as to indicate "ontology in the psychological area: the capacity for self-relationship constitutes the genus *Homo sapiens*."[39]

From a different perspective Desmond Morris reaches the same conclusion—"Face-to-face sex is 'personalized sex'"—for much the same reason: To a self-conscious, relationship-forming species such as ours, the identity of the sexual partner is much more important than it is to species who mate primarily on the basis of chemical attraction. And the frontal approach keeps the sexual stimuli and gratification from the

38. *The Psychology of Sex*, p. 27.
39. *Love and Will*, pp. 311, 312.

partner and his or her *personal* identity closely connected.[40]   Again,
sexuality and personality are seen to be inextricably interrelated.

Personalism

The second major misunderstanding of human sexuality results from
a failure to grant *enough* importance to the *bodily* component of the
dialectic, with too great an emphasis upon the "personality."   This
position is well illustrated by radical Protestant personalism.[41]   In this
view, which is strongly reminiscent of Manichaeanism, a person can do
virtually anything that is desired for self-fulfillment without regard to
any integrity which may be claimed for the body on its own account.
Although the body is not necessarily considered to be inherently evil,
it is thought to exist *solely* as a slave of the personality.   Thus, the self
can do whatever it wants, without any sense of obligation to the organs
and systems themselves, since their own inherent integrity and purpose—irrespective of the uses to which the individual wants to put
them—are denied.   Once again the tension of the dialectic is lost.

A clear example of the extremes to which this view can be taken is
the position adopted by some radical feminists.   Shulamith Firestone,
for example, presents as "the first demand for any alternative system . . .
the freeing of women from the tyranny of their reproductive biology
by every means available."   She strongly advocates the rapid development of artificial reproduction because "*pregnancy is barbaric* . . . the
temporary deformation of the body of the individual for the sake of
the species.   Moreover, childbirth *hurts*.   And it isn't good for you."[42]
More generally, she anticipates the day when "a healthy transsexuality
would be the norm."   In an excellent statement of her disregard of
any integrity which might be inherent in the body for the sake of a
suprabiological goal, Firestone says,

40. *The Naked Ape*, p. 62.

41. Terminology is a bit of a problem here.   The word I have chosen, *personalism*, is given to prolix meanings, of which I am aware.   Nevertheless, it seems to
say best what I intend, as explicated in the text, with less misunderstanding (and
clearer contrast to *naturalism*) than some other possible terms, e.g., *subjec-
tivism* or *spiritualism*, the second of which connotes an other-worldly, ascetic
outlook to many.   The personalism which I intend is not other-worldly or ascetic
in the usual sense but merely fails to recognize the necessary importance of our
existence as bodily-biological beings, a state of existence which places inherent
limits on what we can do as "persons."

42. *The Dialectic of Sex: The Case for the Feminist Revolution* (New York:
Bantam Books, 1970), pp. 206, 198.

> All other things being equal, people might still prefer those of the opposite sex simply because it is more convenient. But even this is a large assumption. For if sexuality were indeed at no time separated from other responses, if one individual responded to the other in a total way that merely included sexuality as one of its components, then it is unlikely that a *purely physical factor* could be decisive.[43]

In short, the bodily, biological aspect of sexuality can be readily denied in order to further individual self-fulfillment, or to avoid discomfort.

Another specific instance of this separation of man's sexuality from his body through the failure to accept the necessary biological element in the dialectic is found in Herbert Richardson's conclusions in *Nun, Witch, Playmate*. He advocates a move toward "less genitality" in our sexual self-understanding and a "heightened control over the instinctual sexual processes by the human intelligence and will."[44] Such control is, of course, what has been suggested earlier in this book as the distinguishing mark of *human* sexuality, but Richardson goes to such an extreme that he denies the necessary recognition of the integrity of the biological, bodily base of our sexuality. He claims that "sexual intercourse does not require the final stage of orgasm, and that the process of sexual union is *so at man's command* that he can choose or withhold orgasm at any point."[45] Referring to the ecstatic dancing of the Shakers (who "explicitly renounced" coital intercourse), Richardson asserts that "it is an intrinsically superior mode of sexual interaction of which ordinary intercourse is but an inferior anticipation." He concludes that "the Shakers, by their celibacy, found their way into a higher, more complex, more satisfying form of sex." Finally, he states that the Mormon idea of "celestial marriage" shows that sex and procreation are spiritual acts and not essentially biological.[46]

I certainly do not want to deny the importance of the spiritual dimension of human sexuality; it is, after all, *one* of the sides of the dialectic. Nor am I interested in questioning the validity of the experiences of the Shakers, Mormons, or any other group. But Richardson's views—which he advocates as guidelines for the direction the further evolution of our sexuality should take—do illustrate a con-

43. *Ibid.*, pp. 58–59; italics added.
44. P. 133.
45. *Ibid.*, italics added. He is citing with hearty approval the view of John Humphrey Noyes, founder of the Oneida Community.
46. *Ibid.*, pp. 129, 130, 131, 134.

temporary denial of the integrity and necessity of the biological, bodily aspect of sexuality under the guise of a heightened concern for the "real person." Our sexuality is surely more than a natural, somatic function, but it is also undeniably bodily.

One must ask if the move toward "less genitality," toward greater rational control and organization of our sexuality, is not a subtly disguised neo-gnosticism, an unrecognized (or unacknowledged) discomfort with man's nature as a bodily sexual being (whose sexuality is surely *genital* in a basic sense). If this is indeed the motivation behind such suggestions, then they are to be rejected on both scientific and theological grounds. Biological research has shown us that we are embodied, with a certain integrity of purpose and function residing in our various organs; and the same God who "created them male and female" intended and sanctioned the use of the organs that make them so, as is celebrated in the Wisdom literature, affirmed by Jesus, and acknowledged even by Paul.

Similarly, the current demand to treat everyone as "human beings," as "persons," rather than as men and women is in fact also neo-gnosticism, a return to a docetic view of man: It implicitly rejects our essential created nature as *sexual* beings in favor of a "personality" to be fulfilled; and it fails to acknowledge our inescapable physical existence, especially our sexuality. The truth is that one's personality can *never* be fulfilled without an abiding consciousness of sexuality because it is one of the primary elements in making one who one is and is a keystone in establishing one's very personality. The personality to be realized simply cannot be separated from the sexuality which some advocate ignoring. The answer, then, lies not in denying our sexuality, but in affirming it for the purposes for which it was intended, one of which is the most intimate communion possible between two *different* beings. In this intimacy, paradoxically, the two both know most clearly that they *are* different and yet also realize that on the deepest spiritual and personal level this difference is irrelevant.

Sexuality as Participant

In opposition both to those who would define human sexuality only in terms of its bodily manifestations and to those who would deny the necessary importance of its biological dimension, we affirm once again the dialectical interdependence of *both* elements. The result of this affirmation might be called—maintaining the dialectic—a view of *sexuality as participant*. That is, man is participant in sexuality (not merely in the sex act but in sexuality itself), while at the same time sexuality is participant in humanity (a constitutive element in what makes man human). Biological sexuality, without the unique mental-spiritual characteristics which man displays, does not reach the full potential for communication, relationship, and pleasure of which it is capable; but man, as seen both biologically and biblically, is only fully understood as human in recognition and affirmation of his nature as a sexual being.

From the Christian perspective, the ultimate example of the dialectical unity that is man—the Incarnation—provides support for this particular understanding of human sexuality. Christians affirm that in this action God—the Supreme Spirit—"became flesh" and existed as a human being, with all that this implies. Unfortunately, as Conrad Bonifazi points out, "the religion of the *incarnate* Word," with its emphasis on the natural and the material, quickly fell prey to an "ascetic virus," which stressed the supernatural and denigrated the material. This subordination of the natural "makes nonsense of the whole concept of Incarnation whereby the New Testament wished to affirm that the God who is personal Love is indissolubly united not only with the human race but also with the entire universe of matter."[47]

With specific reference to sexuality, this is of course a conclusion which we have already seen to be strongly supported in the Old Testament, both in its explicit teachings (particularly the Genesis creation accounts and the Song of Songs) and in its overall attitude: We *are* sexual beings, and our sexuality is an integral part of our personal identity and of our humanity. It is not just a bothersome appendage, an afterthought of the Creator, which obstructs our "real selves," our "souls" or intellects. Indeed, in Hebrew religion the *true* identity of the individual was unavoidably linked in an obvious sense with his sexuality (through the ritual of circumcision), and the only way that he could perpetuate that identity—that he could continue to exist—was also sexual, through the begetting of offspring.

In the New Testament, we found that both Jesus and Paul affirmed

47. "Biblical Roots of an Ecologic Conscience," in Michael Hamilton, ed., *This Little Planet* (New York: Charles Scribner's Sons, 1970), pp. 205–06.

the Old Testament attitude toward the goodness of sexuality rightly expressed. Paul went so far as to assert that the body is the "temple of the Holy Spirit" and that through marital coitus an unbeliever can be brought into right relationship with God by a believing spouse. Underlying all of this, of course, is an incarnational view of reality.

The Incarnation, if its implications had been kept fully in mind, would have provided for Christian thought the means and example par excellence for overcoming the body/mind dualism which has been the source of so many problems. It is necessary, then, to regain the biblical understanding of Incarnation and the faith that it undergirds, which, as Temple says, "is the most avowedly materialist of all the great religions." Indeed, the central affirmation of Christianity is that "the Word was made flesh," and Temple thinks the last word was selected deliberately because of its specifically materialistic implications. In short, "by the very nature of its central doctrine Christianity is committed to a belief in the ultimate significance of the historical process, and in the reality of matter and its place in the divine scheme."[48]

By its self-avowed materialism, therefore, Christianity affirms the human body, which God saw fit not only to create but to celebrate as the means for the ultimate revelation of his redeeming love for our world through the "embodiment" of his Son Jesus Christ. The goodness of the material world (including the human body and sexuality) proclaimed at creation is strikingly affirmed through the Incarnation. Once and for all, any dualistic view of the body as evil and less valuable than the soul has been laid to rest, and the Christian can affirm the body and therefore human sexuality, neither solely as a "natural" phenomenon nor as a regrettable necessity, but as a God-given gift to be used responsibly and to be enjoyed.

48. *NMG*, p. 478.

Glossary for Chapters 5 and 6

ADRENOGENITAL SYNDROME   A condition transmitted as a recessive genetic trait in which the adrenal gland produces an excess amount of masculinizing hormone during the fetal period and thereafter, unless corrected by cortisone therapy.   In females, the genitals are ambiguous and require surgical feminization.

ANDROGEN   A collective name for the male hormones, i.e., those hormones that have a masculinizing action.

ANLAGE(N)   The initial tissues in the embryo or fetus that develop and differentiate into a more complex structure; cf. *primordia*.

CHROMOSOMES   The threadlike or rod-shaped bodies in the cell nucleus that carry the genes (q.v.); the normal human cell contains 46 chromosomes arranged in 23 pairs except for the gametes, which have only 23 chromosomes.

COITUS   Sexual intercourse.

CORTEX   In anatomy, the outer layer or segment of an internal organ, especially the layer of gray matter over most of the brain (neocortex); contrasted with *medulla*.

DEVELOPMENTAL VARIABLES   Factors that enter into the psychosexual maturation of the individual; in the order in which the variables make their major contribution to psychosexual differentiation, they are as follows:

1. GENETIC or CHROMOSOMAL SEX   Determination of normal differentiation as male or female by the chromosomal pattern (XY or XX, respectively) that results when ovum and sperm unite.

2. GONADAL SEX   Differentiation of testes or ovaries, with consequent production of their specific hormones.

3. HORMONAL SEX   Production of androgen by the testes and estrogen by the ovaries, leading to appropriate morphological differentiation and later reproductive capability.

4. INTERNAL MORPHOLOGIC SEX   Differentiation of the internal sexual organs: uterus, fallopian tubes, and vagina in the female; vas deferens, seminal vesicles, and ejaculatory ducts in the male.

5. EXTERNAL MORPHOLOGIC SEX   Differentiation of the external genitalia.

6. HYPOTHALAMIC SEX   Differentiation according to sex of the hypothalamus, that portion of the brain primarily responsible for the mediation of reproductive behavior.

7. SEX OF ASSIGNMENT and REARING   Determination of sex by examination of the external genitals at birth, and rearing in accord with the particular society's expectations for an individual of that sex.

133

DIMORPHISM   Possessing two forms, such as male and female; the term usually refers to bodily structure but can be generalized to include behavior, attitudes, and any traits that may differ in the two forms.

EMBRYO   The unborn offspring of an animal during the earliest stages of development within the uterus; in the human the embryonic period comprises the first eight weeks.

ENDOCRINE TIMING   The determination of sexual drive and receptivity by cyclical release of hormones into the blood, as during an animal's estrus or rut, with little or no control by psychological/emotional factors.

ENDOCRINOLOGY   The study of the ductless glands (e.g., pituitary, testes, ovaries) and their characteristic chemical substances, hormones, which are secreted directly into the bloodstream, and of the effects of these hormones on metabolic processes.

ETHOLOGY   The study of animals and their interactions in their natural environment; in human ethology, man is seen as a member of the animal kingdom and the origin of human behavior is sought in infrahuman primates.

ESTROUS   Pertaining to a cyclical period of sexual receptivity in the female animal, characterized by intense sexual drive and changes in the sexual organs.

FETUS   The unborn young of an animal during the later stages of development within the uterus; in the human, the embryo becomes a fetus at the age of eight weeks.

GAMETES   Reproductive cells that can unite to begin the process of differentiation that leads to a new individual; in humans, the gametes ("marrying cells") are the ovum and sperm.

GENDER IDENTITY   The self-awareness, conscious or unconscious, that one is male or female.

GENDER ROLE   The overt behavior displayed, to others and to oneself, as a result of one's gender identity as male or female.

GENES   The hereditary elements that are passed from parent to offspring in sexual reproduction; genes are segments of DNA molecules and are carried by the chromosomes.

GONADS   The glands which produce reproductive cells, viz., the ovaries and testes.

HERMAPHRODITE   A person in whom both male and female gonads are present.

HORMONE   A chemical substance secreted by certain organs of the body directly into the bloodstream and carried to another organ or tissue, upon which it has a specific effect.

HYPOTHALAMUS   A small segment of the brain that controls the body's autonomic functions and is most directly involved in regulating the activity of the endocrine system through its control of the pituitary gland, thus exerting considerable influence upon sexual behavior.

INFRAHUMAN   Pertaining to those animals beneath man on the evolutionary scale, especially other primates such as chimpanzees and monkeys.

MEDULLA   In anatomy, the inner portion of an organ; contrasted with *cortex*.

MORPHOLOGY   The form and structure of an organ; in this book, the "shape" of the genitals, internal and external.

NATURE-NURTURE   A controversy over the source of certain differences among individuals of a given race; one position (nature) holds that such differences are innate, predetermined, and thus independent of postnatal influences, while the other position (nurture) maintains that they are not prenatally determined but result from the experiences of growing up; in this book, the nature-nurture debate has to do primarily with behavioral and temperamental differences between males and females of the human race.

NEUROENDOCRINOLOGY   The study of the interdependence of the nervous system and the endocrine system.

NEUTRALITY-AT-BIRTH   A theory of psychosexual development that holds that the infant is psychosexually undifferentiated at birth and only takes on characteristics considered male or female by its culture in the course of growing up.

PHYLETIC   Pertaining to a given phylum or race; phyletic elements in human behavior are those shared by all members of the human race in contrast to those which belong only to individuals or certain groups.

PHYLOGENETIC   Pertaining to the history or evolutionary development of a plant or animal species.

PHYSIOLOGY   The study of the functions and processes of living organisms, especially of their various organs and parts; contrasted with *anatomy*, the study of the structure of organisms.

PRIMORDIA   In embryology, the original structure or tissue from which more developed structures arise; cf. *anlage*.

PSEUDOHERMAPHRODITE   A person in whom the gonads of one sex are present but whose external appearance is of the opposite sex.

TESTOSTERONE   The major androgen (male hormone), secreted by the cells of the testes, which functions to produce and maintain male secondary sex characteristics.

Bibliography

Books

Anderson, Floyd, ed. *A Newsman's View of the Birth Control Encyclical.* St. Meinrad, Ind.: Abbey Press, 1969.

Barbour, Ian. *Issues in Science and Religion.* Englewood Cliffs: Prentice-Hall, Inc., 1966.

Barth, Gerhard. *Tradition and Interpretation in Matthew.* Translated by Percy Scott. Philadelphia: Westminster Press, 1963.

Bauer, Walter. *A Greek-English Lexicon of the New Testament and Other Early Christian Literature.* Translated by William F. Arndt and F. Wilbur Gingrich. Chicago: University of Chicago Press, 1957.

Blenkinsopp, Joseph. *Sexuality and the Christian Tradition.* Dayton, Ohio: Pflaum Press, 1969.

Brueggemann, Walter. *In Man We Trust: The Neglected Side of Biblical Faith.* Richmond: John Knox Press, 1972.

Buber, Martin. *Good and Evil.* New York: Charles Scribner's Sons, 1953.

Burtt, E. A. *The Metaphysical Foundations of Modern Science.* Anchor Books. Rev. ed. Garden City: Doubleday & Company, Inc., 1954.

Chardin, Pierre Teilhard de. *The Phenomenon of Man.* Translated by Bernard Wall. Harper Torchbooks. New York: Harper & Row, 1959.

Childs, Brevard S. *Biblical Theology in Crisis.* Philadelphia: Westminster Press, 1970.

Conzelmann, Hans. *History of Primitive Christianity.* Translated by John E. Steely. Nashville: Abingdon Press, 1973.

Copleston, Frederick. *A History of Philosophy.* Vol. IV: *Descartes to Leibniz.* Garden City: Image Books, 1960.

DeRopp, Robert S. *Sex Energy: The Sexual Force in Man and Animals.* New York: Delacorte Press, 1969.

Descartes, René. *The Philosophical Works of Descartes.* 2 vols. Translated by Elizabeth S. Haldane and G. R. T. Ross. Cambridge: Cambridge University Press, 1931.

Dobzhansky, Theodosius. *Mankind Evolving.* New York: Bantam Books, 1962.

Driver, S. R. *A Critical and Exegetical Commentary on Deuteronomy.* Vol. V of the International Critical Commentary. Edited by S. R. Driver, Alfred Plummer, and C. A. Briggs. New York: Charles Scribner's Sons, 1916.

Ellis, Albert. *The Search for Sexual Enjoyment.* New York: Macfadden-Bartell, 1966.

Epstein, Louis M. *Sex Laws and Customs in Judaism.* New York: Bloch Publishing Co., 1948.

Feine, Paul, and Behm, Johannes. *Introduction to the New Testament.* Completely reedited by Werner Georg Kümmel. Translated by A. J. Mattill, Jr. 14th rev. ed. Nashville: Abingdon Press, 1966.

Firestone, Shulamith. *The Dialectic of Sex: The Case for the Feminist Revolution.* New York: Bantam Books, 1970.

Ford, Clellan S., and Beach, Frank A. *Patterns of Sexual Behavior.* Harper Colophon Books. New York: Harper & Row, 1951.

Francoeur, Robert T. *Utopian Motherhood: New Trends in Human Reproduction.* Garden City: Doubleday & Company, Inc., 1970.

Fuller, Watson, ed. *The Biological Revolution: Social Good or Social Evil?* Anchor Books. Garden City: Doubleday & Company, Inc., 1972.

Furnish, Victor Paul. *Theology and Ethics in Paul.* Nashville: Abingdon Press, 1968.

Gadpaille, Warren J. *The Cycles of Sex.* Edited by Lucy Freeman. New York: Charles Scribner's Sons, 1975.

Handler, Philip, ed. *Biology and the Future of Man.* New York: Oxford University Press, 1970.

Harkness, Georgia. *Women in Church and Society.* Nashville: Abingdon Press, 1972.

Harrelson, Walter. *From Fertility Cult to Worship.* Anchor Books. Garden City: Doubleday & Company, Inc., 1969.

Hutt, Corinne. *Males and Females.* Baltimore: Penguin Books, 1972.

Kinsey, Alfred C.; Pomeroy, Wardell B.; Martin, Clyde E.; and Gebhard, Paul H. *Sexual Behavior in the Human Female.* Pocket Books. New York: Simon & Schuster, Inc., 1965.

Masters, William H., and Johnson, Virginia E., in association with Levin, Robert J. *The Pleasure Bond: A New Look at Sexuality and Commitment.* Boston: Little, Brown and Company, 1974.

May, Rollo. *Love and Will.* New York: W. W. Norton & Company, Inc., 1969.

Mead, Margaret. *Male and Female: A Study of the Sexes in a Changing World.* Laurel Edition. New York: Dell Publishing Co., Inc., 1949.

———. *Sex and Temperament in Three Primitive Societies.* Mentor Books. New York: New American Library, 1935.

Merleau-Ponty, Maurice. *Phenomenology of Perception.* Translated by Colin Smith. London: Routledge & Kegan Paul, 1962.

Money, John. *Sex Errors of the Body: Dilemmas, Education, Counseling.* Baltimore: Johns Hopkins University Press, 1968.

———, and Ehrhardt, Anke A. *Man & Woman, Boy & Girl.* Baltimore: Johns Hopkins University Press, 1972.

Morris, Desmond. *The Naked Ape.* New York: Dell Publishing Co., Inc., 1967.

Pascal, Blaise. *Pensées: Thoughts on Religion and Other Subjects.* Translated by William F. Trotter. Edited by H. S. Thayer and Elisabeth B. Thayer. New York: Washington Square Press, Inc., 1965.

Pedersen, Johannes. *Israel: Its Life and Culture,* 2 vols. London: Oxford University Press, 1926.

Phipps, William E. *The Sexuality of Jesus: Theological and Literary Perspectives.* New York: Harper & Row, 1973.

——. *Was Jesus Married?: The Distortion of Sexuality in the Christian Tradition.* New York: Harper & Row, 1970.

Rad, Gerhard von. *Genesis: A Commentary.* Translated by John H. Marks. Philadelphia: Westminster Press, 1961.

——. *Old Testament Theology.* 2 vols. Translated by D. M. G. Stalker. New York: Harper & Row, 1962.

Ramsey, Paul. *Fabricated Man: The Ethics of Genetic Control.* A Yale Fastback. New Haven: Yale University Press, 1970.

Reik, Theodor. *The Creation of Woman: A Psychoanalytic Inquiry into the Myth of Eve.* New York: McGraw-Hill Book Company, 1960.

Renckens, Henricus. *Israel's Concept of the Beginning: The Theology of Genesis 1–3.* New York: Herder and Herder, 1964.

Richardson, Herbert. *Nun, Witch, Playmate.* New York: Harper & Row, 1971.

Robinson, II. Wheeler. *Corporate Personality in Ancient Israel.* Facet Books. Philadelphia: Fortress Press, 1964.

Schnackenburg, Rudolf. *The Moral Teaching of the New Testament.* Translated by J. Holland-Smith and W. J. O'Hara. New York: Herder & Herder, 1965.

Schwarz, Oswald. *The Psychology of Sex.* Pelican Books. Baltimore: Penguin Books, 1949.

Smith, Harmon L. *Ethics and the New Medicine.* Nashville: Abingdon Press, 1970.

Speiser, E. A. *Genesis.* Vol. I of the Anchor Bible. Edited by William F. Albright and David N. Freedman. Garden City: Doubleday & Company, Inc., 1964.

Stoller, Robert J. *Sex and Gender: On the Development of Masculinity and Femininity.* New York: Science House, 1968.

Temple, William. *Christianity in Thought and Practice.* New York: Morehouse Publishing Co., 1936.

——. *Christus Veritas.* London: Macmillan & Co Ltd, 1949.

——. *Nature, Man and God.* London: Macmillan & Co Ltd, 1964.

Thielicke, Helmut. *The Ethics of Sex.* Translated by John W. Doberstein. New York: Harper & Row, 1964.

Westermann, Claus. *The Genesis Accounts of Creation.* Translated by Norman E. Wagner. Facet Books. Philadelphia: Fortress Press, 1964.

Articles

Beach, Frank A. "Experimental Studies of Mating Behavior in Animals." *Sex Research: New Developments.* Edited by John Money. New York: Holt, Rinehart and Winston, 1965, pp. 113–34.

Bonifazi, Conrad. "Biblical Roots of an Ecological Conscience." *This Little Planet.* Edited by Michael Hamilton. New York: Charles Scribner's Sons, 1970, pp. 203–33.

Bronowski, Jacob. "Technology and Culture in Evolution." *The American Scholar,* 41 (Spring, 1972), 197–211.

Buchanan, George Wesley. "The Old Testament Meaning of the Knowledge of Good and Evil." *Journal of Biblical Literature*, 75 (June, 1956), 114–20.

Davies, W. D. "Law in the NT." *The Interpreter's Dictionary of the Bible.* K–Q. New York: Abingdon Press, 1962, 95–102.

———. "The Relevance of the Moral Teaching of the Early Church." *Neotestamentica et Semitica: Studies in Honour of Matthew Black.* Edited by E. Earle Ellis and Max Wilcox. Edinburgh: T. & T. Clark, 1969, pp. 30–49.

Diamond, Milton. "A Critical Evaluation of the Ontogeny of Human Sexual Behavior." *The Quarterly Review of Biology*, 40 (June, 1965), 147–75.

Driver, Tom. "Sexuality and Jesus." *New Theology No. 3.* Edited by Martin E. Marty and Dean G. Peerman. New York: Macmillan Company, 1966, pp. 118–32.

Gordis, Robert. "The Knowledge of Good and Evil in the Old Testament and the Qumran Scrolls." *Journal of Biblical Literature*, 76 (June, 1957), 123–38.

Gottwald, N. K. "Song of Songs." *The Interpreter's Dictionary of the Bible.* R–Z. New York: Abingdon Press, 1962, 420–26.

Hampson, John, and Hampson, Joan. "The Ontogenesis of Sexual Behavior in Man." *Sex and Internal Secretions.* Edited by W. C. Young. 3rd ed. 2 vols. Baltimore: Williams & Williams Co., 1961, II, 1401–32.

Levine, Seymour. "Sex Differences in the Brain." *Scientific American*, (April, 1966), 84–90.

McKenzie, John L. "The Literary Characteristics of Genesis 2–3." *Theological Studies*, 15 (December, 1954), 541–72.

Mead, Margaret. "Cultural Determinants of Sexual Behavior." *Sex and Internal Secretions.* Edited by W. C. Young. 3rd ed. 2 vols. Baltimore: Williams & Williams Co., 1961, II, 1433–79.

Money, John. "Sex Hormones and Other Variables in Human Eroticism." *Sex and Internal Secretions.* Edited by W. C. Young. 3rd ed. 2 vols. Baltimore: Williams & Williams Co., 1961, II, 1383–1400.

Murphy, Roland E. "Form-Critical Studies in the Song of Songs." *Interpretation*, XXVII (October, 1973), 413–22.

Oepke, Albrecht. "γυνή." *Theological Dictionary of the New Testament.* Vol. I. Edited by Gerhard Kittel. Translated by Geoffrey W. Bromiley. Grand Rapids: Eerdmans Publishing Company, 1964, 776–89.

Orr, William F. "Paul's Treatment of Marriage in 1 Corinthians 7." *Pittsburgh Perspective*, VII (September, 1967), 5–22.

Porteous, N. W. "Man, Nature of, in the OT." *The Interpreter's Dictionary of the Bible.* K–Q. New York: Abingdon Press, 1962, 242–46.

Raisman, Geoffrey, and Field, Pauline M. "Sexual Dimorphism in the Preoptic Area of the Rat." *Science*, 173 (August 20, 1971), 731–33.

Scroggs, Robin. "Paul and the Eschatological Woman: Revisited." *Journal of the American Academy of Religion*, XLII (September, 1974), 532–37.

Sherfey, Mary Jane. "The Evolution and Nature of Female Sexuality in Relation to Psychoanalytic Theory." *Journal of the American Psychoanalytic Association*, 14 (January, 1966), 28–128.

Simpson, Cuthbert. "Genesis: Exegesis." *The Interpreter's Bible.* Vol. I. New York: Abingdon Press, 1952, 465–829.

Sloan, Don. "Answers to Questions." *Medical Aspects of Human Sexuality*, VII (January, 1973), 10.

Smart, James D. "Hosea (Man and Book)." *The Interpreter's Dictionary of the Bible.* E–J. New York: Abingdon Press, 1962, 648–53.

Stern, Herold S. "The Concept of Chastity in Biblical Society." *Journal of Sex Research,* 2 (July, 1966), 89–97.

Weiss, Charles. "Motives for Male Circumcision among Preliterate and Literate People." *Journal of Sex Research,* 2 (July, 1966), 69–88.

Young, W. C., Goy, Robert W., and Phoenix, Charles H. "Hormones and Sexual Behavior." *Science,* 143 (January 17, 1964), 212–18.